Welcome

From its roots in the southern Appalachian mountains, what we know today as country grew from a distinctive mix of folk, blues, bluegrass and more to become one of the defining genres of American music. Country has evolved over multiple generations of artists, but the importance of storytelling has remained at its heart for the past 100 years.

This book celebrates the work of some of the genre's greatest storytellers, whose songs have stood the test of time and whose influence can be felt to this day. Discover the stories of the many kings and queens of country, from innovators like Jimmie Rodgers and Hank Williams to chart-topping legends like Dolly Parton and Shania Twain. Alongside these icons, we also salute the modern country artists – such as Morgan Wallen, Lainey Wilson, Luke Combs and Kacey Musgraves – whose fresh takes are opening up the genre to a whole new audience of fans around the world.

Contents

OVER 60 COUNTRY LEGENDS

INTRODUCTION

8 *A journey across country*
INSIDE THE FASCINATING HISTORY OF THIS POPULAR GENRE

14 *Welcome to Nashville*
HOW MUSIC CITY BECAME THE HOME OF COUNTRY MUSIC

18 *Country detours*
WHEN MAINSTREAM ARTISTS HAVE 'GONE COUNTRY'

COUNTRY ICONS

MEET SOME OF THE GENRE'S PIONEERING, BESTSELLING AND LEGENDARY ARTISTS

- 24 George Strait
- 28 Patsy Cline
- 29 Alan Jackson
- 30 Jimmie Rodgers
- 32 Buck Owens
- 33 Conway Twitty
- 34 The Carter Family
- 36 Willie Nelson
- 37 Kenny Chesney
- 38 Johnny Cash
- 42 Jim Reeves
- 44 Jerry Lee Lewis
- 45 Kris Kristofferson
- 46 Charley Pride
- 48 Alabama
- 49 Linda Ronstadt
- 50 Merle Haggard
- 52 Dolly Parton
- 56 DeFord Bailey
- 57 John Denver
- 58 Kitty Wells
- 60 The Louvin Brothers
- 61 Brad Paisley
- 62 Reba McEntire
- 64 Garth Brooks
- 68 Toby Keith
- 69 Johnny Rodriguez
- 70 Loretta Lynn
- 72 The Chicks
- 73 Glen Campbell
- 74 George Jones
- 76 Keith Urban
- 77 Emmylou Harris
- 78 Hank Williams
- 82 Kenny Rogers
- 83 Linda Martell
- 84 Tammy Wynette
- 86 Tim McGraw
- 87 Alison Krauss
- 88 Waylon Jennings
- 90 Little Big Town
- 91 Jason Aldean
- 92 Shania Twain

MODERN
Country
★ STARS ★

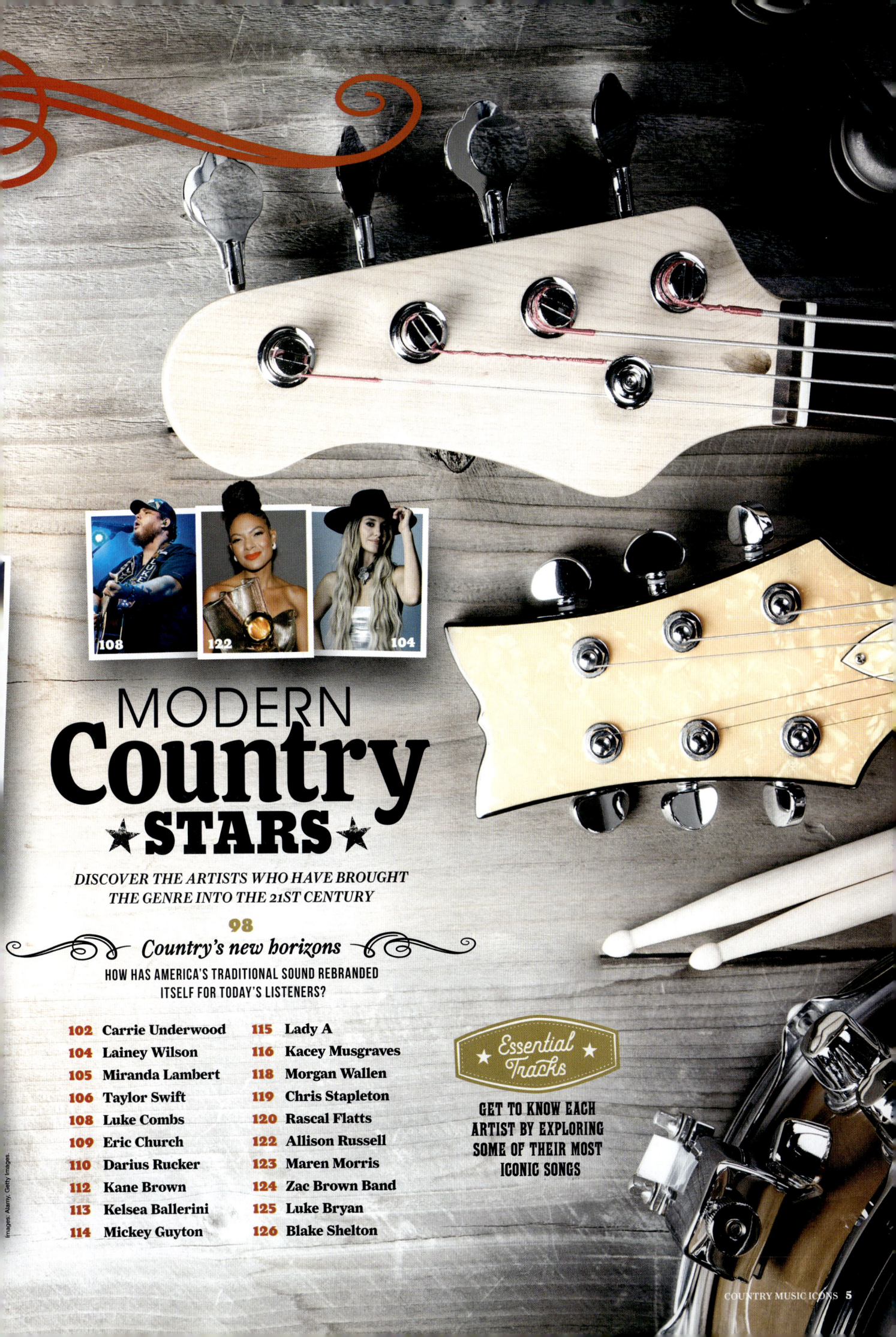

DISCOVER THE ARTISTS WHO HAVE BROUGHT THE GENRE INTO THE 21ST CENTURY

98
Country's new horizons
HOW HAS AMERICA'S TRADITIONAL SOUND REBRANDED ITSELF FOR TODAY'S LISTENERS?

102	Carrie Underwood	**115**	Lady A
104	Lainey Wilson	**116**	Kacey Musgraves
105	Miranda Lambert	**118**	Morgan Wallen
106	Taylor Swift	**119**	Chris Stapleton
108	Luke Combs	**120**	Rascal Flatts
109	Eric Church	**122**	Allison Russell
110	Darius Rucker	**123**	Maren Morris
112	Kane Brown	**124**	Zac Brown Band
113	Kelsea Ballerini	**125**	Luke Bryan
114	Mickey Guyton	**126**	Blake Shelton

Essential Tracks

GET TO KNOW EACH ARTIST BY EXPLORING SOME OF THEIR MOST ICONIC SONGS

INTRODUCTION

8
A journey across country
INSIDE THE FASCINATING HISTORY OF THIS POPULAR GENRE

14
Welcome to Nashville
HOW MUSIC CITY BECAME THE HOME OF COUNTRY MUSIC

18
Country detours
MEET SOME OF THE ARTISTS WHO HAVE 'GONE COUNTRY'

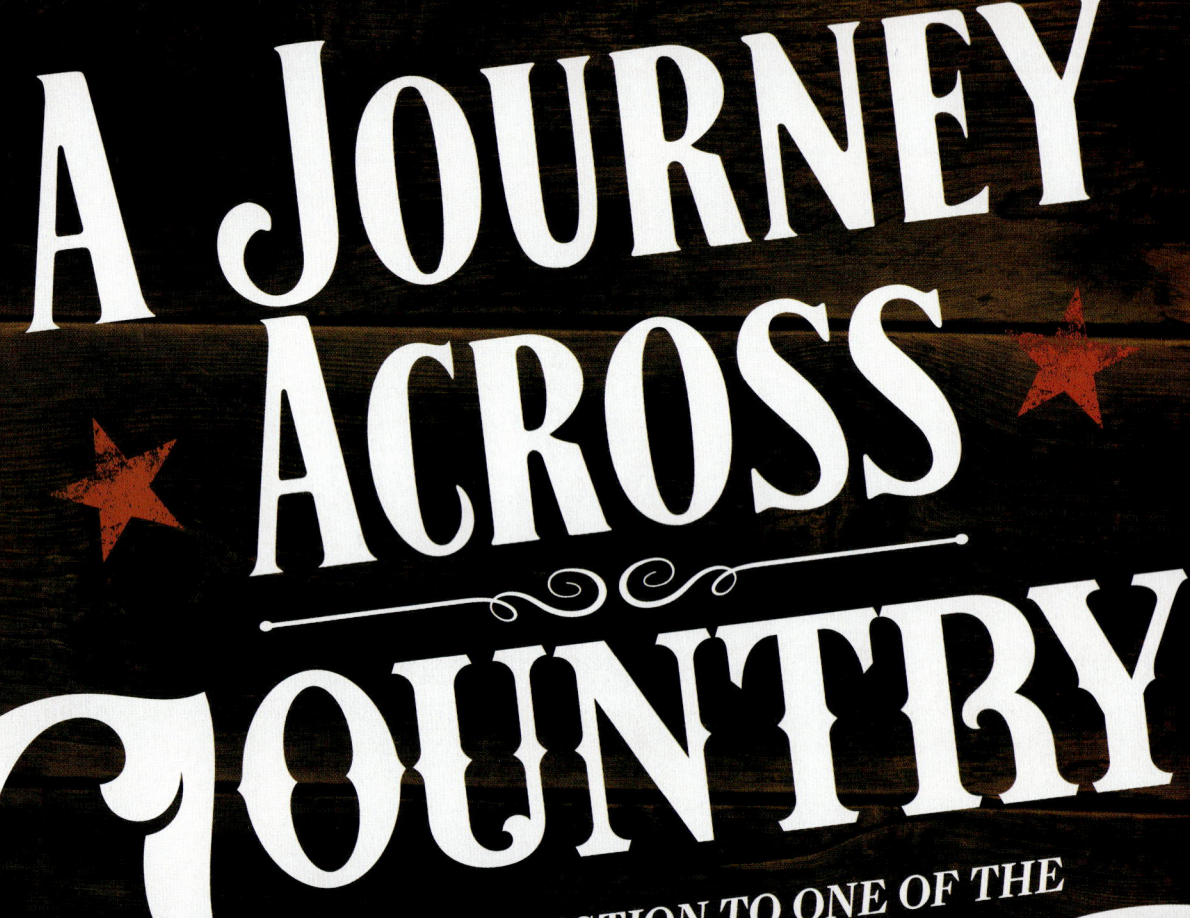

A Journey Across Country

AN INTRODUCTION TO ONE OF THE MOST POPULAR AND DIVERSE GENRES IN AMERICA'S CULTURAL HISTORY

DID YOU KNOW... COUNTRY'S POPULARITY HAS BEEN SURGING — IN 2023, IT WAS ONE OF THE FASTEST-GROWING STREAMING GENRES IN AMERICA.

A JOURNEY ACROSS COUNTRY

When we think of country music, often the first thought that comes to mind is Western landscapes; cowboys racing horses across dirt tracks; and that signature Southern twang. You may have heard the term 'Country & Western', which denotes the melding of styles from the South and Southwest. However, the popular genre has a much more complex and global history, shaped by both African and European influences that date back to the 17th century. The US's diasporic history contributed to what could be argued to be the country's most diverse genre, despite mainstream associations with the working-class white American.

The origins of country can be traced back to English, Scottish and Irish folk ballads, along with the music of African slaves and African-American artists. The style grew out of the Appalachians and the South to become the genre we know today, and was also influenced by the tribal music of Native Americans. It's defined by its string instruments such as the banjo and guitar, and folk harmonies that carry stories over them. It's the same genre that we can see Taylor Swift was influenced by in her own music, weaving tales through each track. The rich tradition of storytelling through song is intrinsically linked to the very landscape country music emerged from, as a destination for travellers both willing and not.

The form of country music that we most commonly think of today first developed a century ago. Folk, fiddles, banjos and blues came together to form early country, then called hillbilly music. This eclectic mixture of influences led to the first official generation of country music. In its time, country music has gone through many faces, perhaps reflective of the itinerant culture of the genre. Country music can be split into six different generations, spanning from the 1920s all the way up to today, when we can even see new styles of the genre emerging in LGBTQ+ spaces.

The second generation welcomed the expansion of the radio, which ultimately gave birth to the Country Airplay charts, where major players in the genre have made their mark on the world.

RIGHT 1922 MARKED THE FIRST COMMERCIAL RECORDINGS OF COUNTRY MUSIC, WITH FIDDLER ALEXANDER "ECK" ROBERTSON.

> ## THE CURRENT GENERATION CONTINUES TO SEE COUNTRY MUSIC EVOLVE

Third-generation country music came to speak to working-class Americans in the 1950s and 1960s, particularly truckers who would journey across the nation. This era also gave birth to the Tulsa sound of blues-rock from Oklahoma, and the Louisiana sound of swamp-pop, created by Cajuns and Creoles. The 1970s and 1980s welcomed iconic country artists such as Waylon Jennings and Willie Nelson, who popularised the subgenre of outlaw country (a resistance to the slick Nashville sound), which came to be defined as the fourth generation. With the fifth generation in the 1990s came international recognition for country-pop, the most prolific subgenre of country music that has crossed over to the mainstream charts. The sixth and current generation of the 21st century continues to see the genre evolve – both musically and socially – as new fusions like country-rap emerged and country culture has started to become more liberal.

BELOW EVENTS LIKE THE COUNTRY TO COUNTRY FESTIVAL (PICTURED) BRING THE GENRE TO A GROWING GLOBAL AUDIENCE OF FANS.

THE BANJO – ASSOCIATED WITH BLUEGRASS AND COUNTRY – EVOLVED FROM INSTRUMENTS BROUGHT OVER BY WEST AFRICAN SLAVES.

10 COUNTRY MUSIC ICONS

A JOURNEY ACROSS COUNTRY

ABOVE COUNTRY MUSIC WAS ALSO POPULARISED BY THE RISE OF WESTERNS IN EARLY- AND MID-20TH-CENTURY CINEMA.

FAR LEFT EARLY BANJOS SUCH AS THIS EXAMPLE HAD BODIES MADE FROM SPLIT GOURDS AND STRETCHED ANIMAL SKINS.

» Queer country: a new generation?

LGBTQ+ people have always existed in country music (see The Sweet Violet Boys, Wilma Burgess, k.d. lang and many more), but 2019 welcomed a potential new generation when Orville Peck, pictured left, released *Pony*. Peck is classic country – a low, distinctive twang over country melodies – but in Peck's world, to borrow a song title, 'Cowboys Are Frequently, Secretly Fond of Each Other'. Queer country-pop may well be influenced by gay club DJs and their long-time love of Shania Twain and Carrie Underwood. The subgenre is highly aesthetic with a viral quality, opening up a new audience to country music.

Country music encompasses a vast range of subgenres, including popular forms such as Americana and bluegrass, to swing and honky tonk. The diversity in subgenres across country music is what originally gave the genre its name. Many regions of the US were influenced in different ways by the same core settlers to create a startling scope of music.

Today, long-standing genres such as rap, rock and pop have merged with country music to create global crossover hits; we only need to look to Beyoncé's *Cowboy Carter* (which broke multiple streaming and chart records around the world) to prove that. Country-pop is the highest-consumed subgenre, with the incredible success of artists like Taylor Swift demonstrating a global thirst for the historic genre's storytelling traits. Country's power lies in its melodic heritage, and the joy of community found through each generation of the genre.

COUNTRY GENERATIONS

» 1920s
'Hillbilly music' was the first commercial iteration of the genre, beginning with fiddlers such as Henry Gilliland and Fiddlin' John Carson. In the late 1920s, Jimmie Rodgers and the Carter Family (both pictured) came onto the scene. Rodgers – who became known as the Father of Country Music – released the hugely successful 'Blue Yodel' in 1927.

1st GENERATION ★ **2nd GENERATION** ★ **3rd GENERATION**

⌃ 1930s-1940s
The Great Depression contributed to a decline in record sales, but also marked the growth of radio, and most notably for country, the Grand Ole Opry, a station born in 1925 that lives on to this day. It was in this age that country picked up more subgenres, including honky tonk, bluegrass and western swing music.

⌃ 1950s-1960s
The influence of 'cowboy' songs took off and merged with country and western, forming the aesthetic we associate with country music today. This generation welcomed New Mexican artists and working-class truckers, as well as the peak of rockabilly – an early form of rock'n'roll influenced by blues and country music, popularised by Elvis Presley.

12 COUNTRY MUSIC ICONS

A JOURNEY ACROSS COUNTRY

🔼 1970s-1980s
The 1970s saw the peak of outlaw country, a subgenre popularised by artists such as Willie Nelson (pictured). The genre brought influences from New Mexico, Texas country, honky tonk and Tejano to name a few. This generation also demonstrated country music's versatility in country-pop and country-rock.

4th GENERATION ★ **5th GENERATION** ★ **6th GENERATION**

🔼 1990s
The expansion of FM radio across rural areas allowed country artists to gain huge commercial success. More female country artists received accolades for their contributions to the genre, and country continued to expand to include alternative subgenres. Artists such as Garth Brooks and Shania Twain took country music global.

🔼 2000s-Present
Country music as we know it today is built of crossovers, with artists successfully merging elements of rock, pop and R&B into the genre. The generation is most closely linked with pop, thanks to artists such as Morgan Wallen (above), Taylor Swift and Carrie Underwood (both pictured top), among other globally successful artists.

WELCOME TO NASHVILLE

Welcome to Nashville

TAKE A TOUR OF MUSIC CITY, TENNESSEE, COUNTRY MUSIC'S SPIRITUAL (AND ACTUAL) HOME

It's said that Tennessee's biggest city, its capital Nashville, first gained the nickname of 'Music City' in 1950, when a local radio DJ named David Cobb used the term on air. Other major centres for music exist in the US, of course (most notably New York, Los Angeles, Philadelphia, Detroit and Chicago), but there's such a concentrated entertainment industry here that the term makes perfect sense – especially, but not only, when we're talking about country music.

Take a look around downtown Nashville next time you're there and you'll see what we mean, from the Country Music Hall of Fame and Museum, the Ryman Auditorium, the Belcourt Theatre, the famous RCA Studios – where the 'Nashville sound' originated – and any number of major and indie record labels. Head nine miles east of downtown and you'll find the greatest of all country music institutions, the Grand Ole Opry. The city isn't just about country, of course: outside that scene there's the Tennessee Performing Arts Center, a major theatre and ballet outlet, and since 2006 the Nashville Symphony Orchestra has resided at the Schermerhorn Symphony Center.

Mind you, those are just the bigger venues: as music fans all know, the real lifeblood of any musical community flows through its smaller bars and clubs, which in Nashville's case cluster in an area around Lower Broadway, Second Avenue and Printer's Alley, collectively referred to as 'the District'. It was there that Nashville first built its reputation as a home for traditional music, with a thriving jazz sound as early as the 1920s in venues such as the Oak Bar and Grille Room in the Hermitage Hotel. When radio and TV came along, local stations were quick to support their hometown's music: older Nashvillians will remember country-themed TV shows such as *Hee Haw* and *Pop! Goes the Country*.

In recent years, musicians of all stripes have flocked to Nashville to record there, from Kiss and Megadeth to R.E.M. and Kings of Leon, and the city has a prosperous hip-hop and soul scene, although country is still its biggest export. Gospel and other faith-based music flourish there, too. The city supports both new and established musicians with a whole wave of initiatives – the Greater Nashville Artist

ABOVE THE RYMAN AUDITORIUM IS BOTH A ROCK & ROLL HALL OF FAME LANDMARK AND A NATIONAL HISTORIC LANDMARK.

RIGHT MANY BIG NAMES HAVE PERFORMED AT THE UNASSUMING, 90-SEATER BLUEBIRD CAFE, WHICH HOSTS ACOUSTIC PERFORMANCES BY LOCAL SONGWRITERS.

🎵 The studio that gave us 'the sound'

The Nashville Sound – precision-engineered country with strings and layers of vocals – was pioneered by RCA Studio B in Music Row, built in 1957 and initially known as RCA Victor Studio. By the end of the 60s the sound had been committed to vinyl on songs such as Jim Reeves' 'He'll Have to Go' and Don Gibson's 'Oh Lonesome Me', while Waylon Jennings, Willie Nelson, Dolly Parton and many other country legends have recorded there. It was a hotbed of innovation despite its focus on traditional music, with the 'Nashville number system' – a kind of shorthand for song structures – originating at Studio B, and between 1957 and 1973 the studio was managed by the great Chet Atkins, who produced hundreds of hits there.

WELCOME TO NASHVILLE

LEFT DOWNTOWN NASHVILLE IS HOME TO MANY THRIVING LIVE VENUES WHERE YOU CAN SOAK UP THE SOUNDS OF MUSIC CITY.

ABOVE THE FAMOUS GRAND OLE OPRY BROADCASTS CELEBRATE THEIR 100TH ANNIVERSARY IN 2025.

THERE WAS AN 'OPRYLAND USA' THEME PARK IN NASHVILLE FROM 1972 TO 1997.

BELOW THE COUNTRY MUSIC HALL OF FAME AND MUSEUM HOLDS FASCINATING EXHIBITIONS AND EVENTS THROUGHOUT THE YEAR.

"MUSICIANS OF ALL STRIPES HAVE FLOCKED TO NASHVILLE TO RECORD

Relief Fund, the Songwriters Lifeline, the Music Health Alliance, the Sweet Relief Musicians Fund and many other programmes – and you can witness the next Taylor Swift or Alison Krauss treading the boards for the first time at events such as the annual CMA Music Festival and the Tennessee State Fair.

If all this sounds a bit over-professional, never fear – Nashville is a whole lot of fun to visit. It has a thriving food scene, with restaurants and bars catering to all tastes, including Tennessee speciality barbecues. There are several theatres and related festivals, a Civil War-era historical scene, art galleries and museums, and annual film and fashion weeks. What's more, it's a hugely popular destination for bachelor and bachelorette parties. One study counted 33 such parties on a single Friday night in 2017 – so whatever your area of interest, you can rely on your visit to Music City being a total blast from start to finish.

COUNTRY MUSIC ICONS 17

Country DETOURS

MANY ARTISTS FROM OTHER GENRES HAVE 'GONE COUNTRY' – OR SOON PLAN TO – DURING THEIR CAREERS. HERE ARE A FEW NOTABLE EXAMPLES...

Ray Charles
MODERN SOUNDS IN COUNTRY & WESTERN MUSIC, 1962

The R&B icon made the album full of country hits after signing a new deal with the label ABC-Paramount. The album is proof of Charles's prowess as a uniquely versatile artist. Ray Charles created a country album that revolutionised crossovers to country, particularly in a time that racially segregated even music genres, such as country, from R&B.

Post Malone
'PICKUP MAN', 2023; F-1 TRILLION, 2024

In 2023, Post Malone made it onto the Country Airplay charts for the first time with a duet version of Joe Diffie's song 'Pickup Man'. He performed the song live with Morgan Wallen and HARDY to pay tribute to Diffie, who died in 2020. With the 2024 country-pop smash hit 'I Had Some Help' (another collaboration with Wallen) and 'Pour Me a Drink' (with Blake Shelton), Malone has all but confirmed the rumours that his upcoming album, *F-1 trillion*, will be a country record.

COUNTRY DETOURS

›› Beyoncé
COWBOY CARTER, 2024

Beyoncé made huge waves in 2024 with her country album. It marks the second in the purported 'Renaissance' trilogy. This was another step in Beyoncé's work to demonstrate and celebrate the power of Black artists' historic influence across all music genres. The name is possibly a nod to the Carter family as well as her duo with Jay-Z.

AFRICAN-AMERICAN MUSICIAN LESLEY RIDDLE SHAPED COUNTRY MUSIC THROUGH HIS TUTELAGE AND INFLUENCE ON THE CARTER FAMILY.

⌃ Lana Del Rey
LASSO, 2024

After releasing a cover of John Denver's 'Take Me Home, Country Roads' in 2023, Del Rey later announced that she was making a country record, called *Lasso*, scheduled for September 2024. It will be the tenth studio album in her illustrious career, and there are rumours it may even include a collaboration with the Queen of Country herself, Dolly Parton, after they were pictured together.

›› Bob Dylan
NASHVILLE SKYLINE, 1969

Nashville Skyline was in no way the first or last exploration Bob Dylan made into country music, but it's arguably the record where he most engaged with the genre. Recorded in the home of the genre, Nashville, it was his ninth studio album and was highly critically acclaimed. The record has been credited for helping to launch the country-rock subgenre.

COUNTRY MUSIC ICONS 19

» Tina Turner
TINA TURNS THE COUNTRY ON!, 1974

Tina Turns the Country On! was Tina Turner's first solo studio record, and it earned her a Grammy nomination in the Best R&B Vocal Performance, Female category. The album mainly features covers, including hits made famous by Kris Kristofferson and Dolly Parton. Despite positive reviews, it never charted and was never released on CD – although you can find it on streaming platforms.

« Cyndi Lauper
DETOUR, 2016

The 'Girls Just Wanna Have Fun' singer is better known for her pop hits, but over the years Cyndi Lauper has often mentioned her love of country. In 2016, she released her 12th album, *Detour*, to pay homage to the genre. Recorded in Nashville, it featured guest appearances from a few country icons, including Willie Nelson, Alison Krauss and Emmylou Harris.

COUNTRY DETOURS

❯❯ Lil Nas X
'OLD TOWN ROAD', 2018

Lil Nas X's debut single 'Old Town Road' blew up in 2018, becoming a huge hit for its unique style that fused country and rap – a relatively rare mix. The artist also released a remix featuring Billy Ray Cyrus. The track gave Lil Nas X the boost to become a major player in the pop industry, despite his biggest hit being distinctly country.

BILLBOARD CONTROVERSIALLY REMOVED 'OLD TOWN ROAD' FROM THEIR COUNTRY CHART, DEEMING IT "NOT COUNTRY ENOUGH".

❮❮ Lionel Richie
TUSKEGEE, 2012

Lionel Richie's tenth album, *Tuskegee*, was a reimagining of his previous hits – this time recorded with country artists. The collaborations included Willie Nelson on 'Easy', and Shania Twain on 'Endless Love'. Richie and his featured guests received praise for the album, which made it to number one in the US on both the *Billboard* 200 and Top Country Albums charts.

❯❯ Ringo Starr
BEAUCOUPS OF BLUES, 1970

As the album's name hints, the second solo studio album by former Beatle Ringo Starr draws on country and western elements throughout. It was recorded in Nashville, a cultural heart of country music. Ringo Starr had been a longtime fan of the genre, encouraging The Beatles to move toward country themselves on *Beatles for Sale* in 1964.

COUNTRY MUSIC ICONS 21

COUNTRY ICONS

MEET SOME OF THE GENRE'S PIONEERING, BESTSELLING AND LEGENDARY ARTISTS

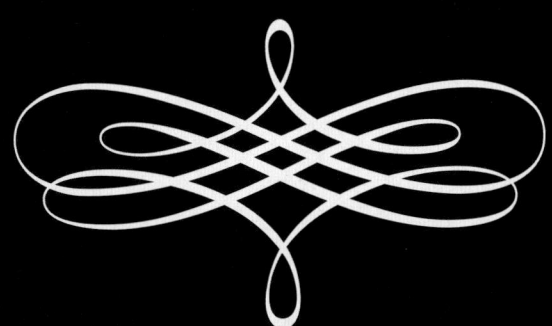

- **24** George Strait
- **28** Patsy Cline
- **29** Alan Jackson
- **30** Jimmie Rodgers
- **32** Buck Owens
- **33** Conway Twitty
- **34** The Carter Family
- **36** Willie Nelson
- **37** Kenny Chesney
- **38** Johnny Cash
- **42** Jim Reeves
- **44** Jerry Lee Lewis
- **45** Kris Kristofferson
- **46** Charley Pride
- **48** Alabama
- **49** Linda Ronstadt
- **50** Merle Haggard
- **52** Dolly Parton
- **56** DeFord Bailey
- **57** John Denver
- **58** Kitty Wells
- **60** The Louvin Brothers
- **61** Brad Paisley
- **62** Reba McEntire
- **64** Garth Brooks
- **68** Toby Keith
- **69** Johnny Rodriguez
- **70** Loretta Lynn
- **72** The Chicks
- **73** Glen Campbell
- **74** George Jones
- **76** Keith Urban
- **77** Emmylou Harris
- **78** Hank Williams
- **82** Kenny Rogers
- **83** Linda Martell
- **84** Tammy Wynette
- **86** Tim McGraw
- **87** Alison Krauss
- **88** Waylon Jennings
- **90** Little Big Town
- **91** Jason Aldean
- **92** Shania Twain

1952–PRESENT

George Strait

THIS KING OF COUNTRY MUSIC HAS BEEN A PIONEER, TAKING THE GENRE BACK TO ITS HONKY-TONK ROOTS

Born in Poteet, Texas, on 18 May 1952, country music icon George Strait spent his childhood on his family's ranch in southern Texas, managed by his teacher father, John Byron Strait Sr. When he wasn't riding horses and helping his father with his duties at the ranch, Strait played guitar in a rock band with his classmates. Strait and his high school sweetheart Norma Voss eloped in 1971, and he enlisted in the US Army that same year, performing in an Army-sponsored country band called Rambling Country. His music at the time was heavily influenced by the likes of Bob Wills, George Jones and Hank Williams, and so began his love for the more traditional side of the genre. He then attended Southwest Texas State University to study agriculture and joined another country band called Stoney Ridge.

After little success promoting his music in Nashville, Strait signed a one-song contract with MCA Records in 1981, releasing his single 'Unwound' which reached the number six spot on the Hot Country Songs chart. This allowed him to release more music with the label, including his debut album *Strait Country* (1981), followed by his first number one song, 'Fool Hearted Memory', a year later. Throughout his career, Strait has produced a vast catalogue of music, with his 30th studio album releasing in 2024. He has been wildly successful in the country music charts, with 61 chart-topping songs and 33 platinum certifications.

Strait's music marked a shift from the genre's embrace of pop and led to a resurgence in interest in the more traditional sounds of country music. Widely regarded as 'neotraditional country', his music often includes classic instruments like fiddles and steel guitars. Strait is still regarded as one of country music's biggest icons, and while he retired from touring after the Cowboy Rides Away Tour (2013-2014), he began his popular Las Vegas residency – Strait to Vegas – in 2016.

IN JUNE 2024, STRAIT PERFORMED TO OVER 110,000 FANS IN TEXAS – A RECORD-BREAKING CROWD FOR A TICKETED CONCERT IN AMERICA.

Essential Tracks
- CARRYING YOUR LOVE WITH ME
- CHECK YES OR NO
- AMARILLO BY MORNING

LIFE & CAREER

◄ On the big screen

Strait took on the lead role in the 1992 film *Pure Country*, playing the character Dusty Chandler, a famous country singer who has abandoned his more traditional style of music. The film performed poorly at the box office, grossing $15 million against a budget of $10 million. Despite this, Strait received praise for his performance as Dusty. He later appeared in the sequel, *Pure Country 2: The Gift* as himself.

GEORGE STRAIT

❯ Award winner

In 2010, *Billboard* named Strait the top country music artist of the last 25 years, and it's easy to see why: he's won multiple awards for his incredible critical success, including his first Grammy award for his 2008 album *Troubadour*, his acknowledgement for Top Country Tour at the 2020 *Billboard* Music Awards and a vast array of awards in the country music genre. He was even given an honorary doctoral degree from his alma mater, Texas State University, in 2006.

> ❝ **BILLBOARD NAMED STRAIT THE TOP COUNTRY MUSIC ARTIST OF THE LAST 25 YEARS**

STRAIT WAS INDUCTED INTO THE COUNTRY MUSIC HALL OF FAME IN 2006.

⌄ On the rodeo

Strait has been involved in the cultural side of country music since childhood, and has performed at more than 20 rodeo events. He made his first appearance at one in 1983 while standing in for Eddie Rabbitt, who was too unwell to perform at the Houston Livestock Show and Rodeo. He recorded his own version of the song 'Amarillo by Morning', which is about a rodeo cowboy and his career.

⌃ Charity champion

In recent decades, Strait has dedicated much of his time to causes benefitting military veterans, including his work as spokesperson for the VF Corporation's Wrangler National Patriot scheme, which seeks to raise money for wounded military veterans and their families. Since 2012, Strait has raised more than $5 million for the Troops First Foundation by hosting the annual Vaqueros Del Mar Invitational Golf Tournament and Concert.

COUNTRY MUSIC ICONS 27

PATSY CLINE

1932–1963

"I DON'T LIKE IT AND I AIN'T GONNA RECORD IT," SAID CLINE ON FIRST HEARING 'CRAZY'.

Essential Tracks
- CRAZY
- I FALL TO PIECES
- SWEET DREAMS OF YOU

Patsy Cline

ONE OF THE GREATEST COUNTRY SINGERS OF ALL TIME, CLINE WAS A PROFOUND INSPIRATION FOR COUNTLESS OTHERS

Patsy Cline was one of the greatest singers in the history of country music and among the first country artists to crossover to the mainstream market. Her tragic death in a plane crash in 1963 at the age of 30 elevated her to icon status, but it was a stature already richly deserved by the close of her short life.

Born in Virginia, Cline began recording in the mid-50s, cutting 17 singles of which one, 'Walkin' After Midnight', was a hit. Her style spanned rockabilly but it wasn't until 1960, with producer Owen Bradley, that she recorded her best works, country-pop crossovers steeped in emotion, with lush orchestration. The first was 'I Fall to Pieces' (1961), which reached No.1 in the country charts and No.12 in the pop charts. But the song that really made her name was the Willie Nelson-penned 'Crazy' (1961), which was marked by Cline's achingly emotional delivery. It was a Top 10 hit on the country and pop charts, as was follow-up single 'She's Got You' (1962). 'Sweet Dreams', the Don Gibson penned country ballad, was released in April 1963, weeks after her passing.

Words by Neil Crossley. Image: Getty Images.

ALAN JACKSON

1958–PRESENT

Essential Tracks
- CHATTAHOOCHEE
- LIVIN' ON LOVE
- WHERE WERE YOU (WHEN THE WORLD STOPPED TURNING)

JACKSON'S BIG BREAK CAME WHEN HIS WIFE GAVE GLEN CAMPBELL A COPY OF HER HUSBAND'S DEMO.

ALAN JACKSON

THIS GEORGIA ARTIST HAS STAYED TRUE TO TRADITIONAL COUNTRY AND CARVED OUT ONE OF THE BIGGEST CAREERS IN THE GENRE

Alan Jackson has sold over 75 million records worldwide and notched up 35 No.1 hits on the *Billboard* Hot Country chart with his neo-traditional style, which draws on country music of the 40s, 50s and 60s. While the stadium-selling new country sound took hold in the 90s, Jackson turned towards a more traditional sound.

His hits have included 'I'd Love You All Over Again' (1991), 'Don't Rock the Jukebox' (1991), 'Chattahoochee' (1993) and 'Gone Country' (1994) and a song informed by the 9/11 attacks 'Where Were You (When the World Stopped Turning)' (2002). Other hits included a tribute to his father, 'Drive (For Daddy Gene) and a breezy upbeat duet with Jimmy Buffet called 'It's Five O'Clock Somewhere' (2003).

In the 2010s, Jackson turned to bluegrass and gospel, and in 2014 the performing rights organisation ASCAP presented him with its Heritage Award, recognising him as its most-performed country music songwriter-artist of the past hundred years.

1897–1933

Jimmie Rodgers

THE FOUNDING FATHER OF COUNTRY MUSIC HAD A HUGE INFLUENCE ON GENERATIONS OF ARTISTS TO COME

He was known as 'The Singing Brakeman' and 'America's Blue Yodeler', but the moniker that really summed up pioneering singer-songwriter Jimmie Rodgers was the 'Father of Country Music'. Rodgers combined the traditional folk music of his Southern upbringing with yodelling, the work chants of Black railroad section crews and African-American blues. The result was a rich fusion that laid the sonic foundation of country music.

Born in Meridian, Mississippi, Rodgers worked on the railroad with his father before tuberculosis forced him to quit. In 1927 he decided to make a career in music, so he joined the Tenneva Ramblers band, an outfit that performed throughout the Blue Ridge Mountains. It was here that Rodgers learned of Ralph Peer's field recordings for the Victor Talking Machine Company that were taking place in Bristol, Tennessee. He recorded solo and went on to record a second session in Camden, New Jersey, which produced 'Blue Yodel No. 1 (T for Texas)', a song that catapulted Rodgers to national fame, selling over half a million copies.

He went on to produce over 110 songs for the label, including 'Waiting for a Train', 'In the Jailhouse Now', 'Frankie and Johnny', 'T. B. Blues', 'Miss the Mississippi and You', and the 12 sequels to 'Blue Yodel' for which he was most famous.

Rodgers was a revelation as a performer, imbuing his shows and recordings with humour, personality and emotion. Most of Rodgers' songs were written with collaborators, including his sister-in-law, Elsie McWilliams. He also collaborated with country music greats, such as the Carter Family. But by 1933, his ill health seriously impacted his work and he died after collapsing from a massive haemorrhage in a hotel room in New York.

Jimmie Rodgers left an enduring legacy. The artists who have acknowledged his influence include Lefty Frizzell, Bill Monroe, Roy Rogers, Johnny Cash, Willie Nelson, Merle Haggard, Dolly Parton, Hank Snow, Bob Dylan and Alison Krauss.

In 1961, Rodgers became one of the first artists to be inducted into the Country Music Hall of Fame, which stated that Rodgers had "brought to the emerging genre of 'hillbilly music' a distinctive, colourful personality and a rousing vocal style", one that has "created and defined the role of the singing star in country music".

THE 1929 SHORT FILM *THE SINGING BRAKEMAN* IS REGARDED AS ONE OF THE FIRST MUSIC VIDEOS.

Essential Tracks

- WAITING FOR A TRAIN
- IN THE JAILHOUSE NOW
- BLUE YODEL NO. 9

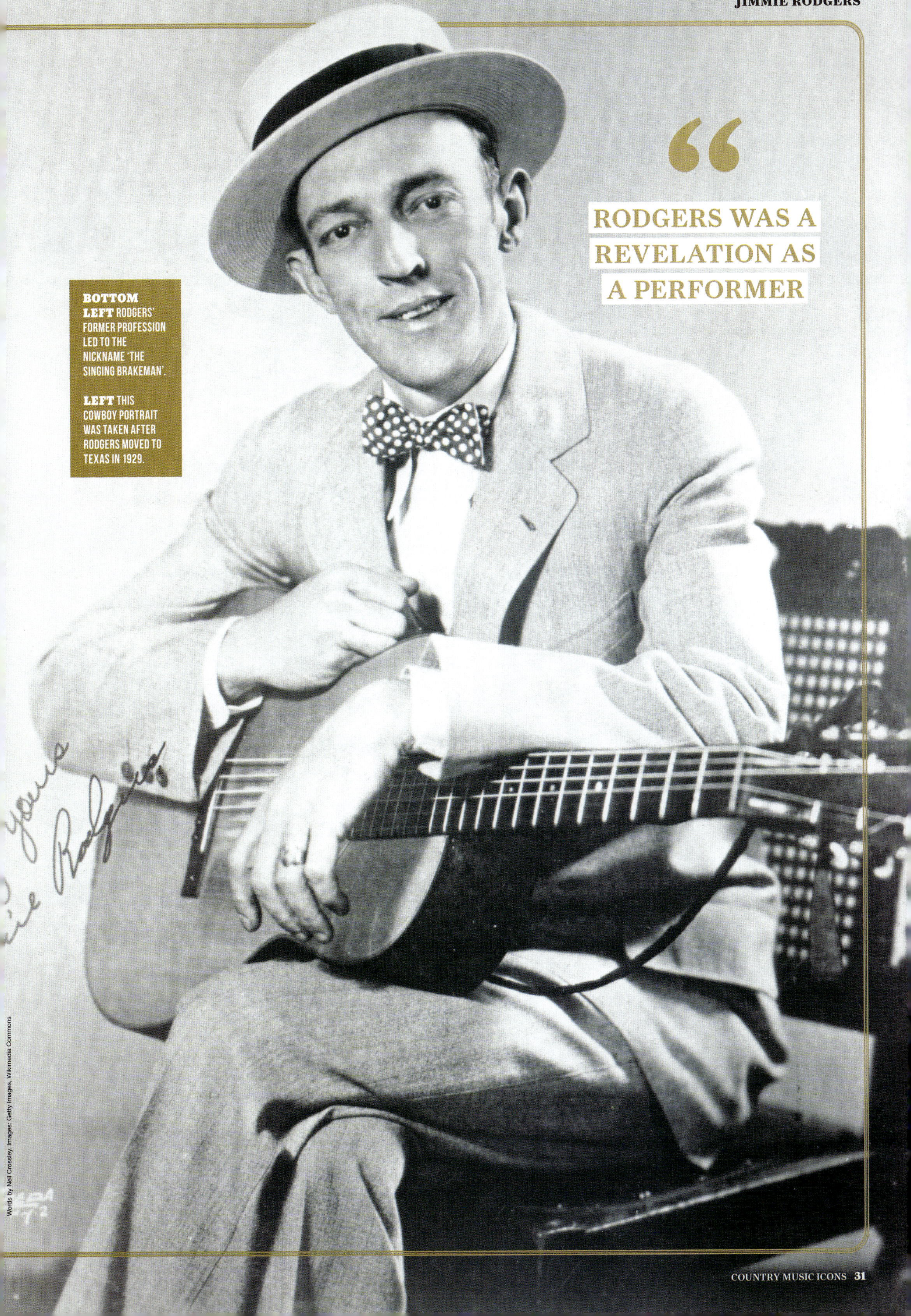

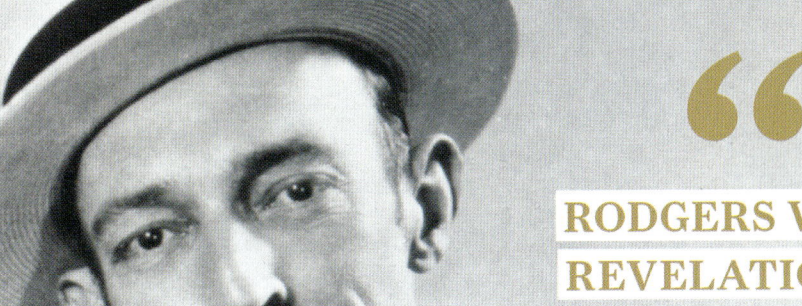

“RODGERS WAS A REVELATION AS A PERFORMER

BOTTOM LEFT RODGERS' FORMER PROFESSION LED TO THE NICKNAME 'THE SINGING BRAKEMAN'.

LEFT THIS COWBOY PORTRAIT WAS TAKEN AFTER RODGERS MOVED TO TEXAS IN 1929.

Words by Neil Crossley. Images: Getty Images, Wikimedia Commons

BUCK OWENS

1929–2006

> OWENS PICKED HIS NAME 'BUCK' WHEN HE WAS A YOUNG CHILD, NAMED AFTER A DONKEY ON THE FAMILY FARM.

Essential Tracks
- ACT NATURALLY
- TOGETHER AGAIN
- WAITIN' IN YOUR WELFARE LINE

OWENS DOMINATED THE COUNTRY CHARTS IN THE MID-60s AND PIONEERED THE DISTINCTIVE, TWANGY BAKERSFIELD SOUND

Texan by birth, Alvis Edgar 'Buck' Owens Jr was a singer, songwriter, guitarist and bandleader who moved to California in 1951 and pioneered what became known as the Bakersfield sound. This was a much more raw, honky-tonk kind of country, different from the string-laden tones emanating from Nashville at the time.

Owens and his band The Buckaroos dominated the country chart of the mid-60s with their clear, twangy sound. Owens' first chart-topping hit was 'Act Naturally', which was later covered by The Beatles in 1965 and sung by Ringo Starr. From 1963 to 1967, Owens released 14 consecutive US Country chart-topping hits, including 'Together Again' (1964), 'I've Got a Tiger by the Tail' ('65), 'Think of Me' ('66), 'Waitin' in Your Welfare Line' ('66) and 'Sam's Place' ('67).

From 1969 to 1986, Owens co-hosted the popular comedy TV variety show *Hee Haw* with fellow musician Roy Clark. His musical achievements are sometimes overlooked, but he laid the foundations for modern country music and inspired whole generations of artists in the process.

Conway Twitty

1933–1993

WITH A CAREER SPANNING FIVE DECADES, THE HIGH PRIEST OF COUNTRY MUSIC BECAME A REIGNING IDOL OF THE INDUSTRY

Born Harold Lloyd Jenkins in Friars Point, Mississippi, Conway Twitty was a country superstar throughout the 70s and 80s, notching up a record 40 No.1 hits over the course of two decades and receiving a string of CMA awards for his duets with Loretta Lynn. He was one of the most successful US artists of the 20th century, selling over 50 million records.

Twitty had a rich, deep, tremulous baritone voice and became one of Nashville's smoothest ballad singers, introducing pop, rock'n'roll and R&B elements into his music. He was also a major songwriting talent, penning 11 of his No.1 hits, and his compositions sometimes featured slightly suggestive themes, which endeared him to an adult audience.

Twitty started out in rock'n'roll and rockabilly, inspired by hearing Elvis Presley's 'Mystery Train' but ultimately became a country artist to his core. It's a lasting testament to Twitty's talent that his stardom endured throughout changing musical fashions across five decades.

Essential Tracks
- LINDA ON MY MIND
- I'D LOVE TO LAY YOU DOWN
- DON'T TAKE IT AWAY

A TALENTED BASEBALL PLAYER, TWITTY WAS OFFERED A CONTRACT BY THE PHILADELPHIA PHILLIES BEFORE BEING DRAFTED.

ACTIVE 1937–1956

THE CARTER FAMILY

THE CARTERS LEARNED TO HARMONISE USING THE SHAPE NOTE SYSTEM, A NOTATION ROOTED IN THE PRE-CIVIL WAR SOUTH.

THE CARTER FAMILY

THE FIRST FAMILY OF COUNTRY MUSIC HAD A SIGNIFICANT INFLUENCE ON THE CREATION AND DEVELOPMENT OF THE GENRE

Of all the artists that Ralph Peer 'discovered' in his legendary recording sessions in Bristol, Tennessee, in 1927, none were more significant than the Carter Family. Widely regarded as 'the First Family of Country Music', they were among the first groups to record commercially produced country music. They created a raft of material from 1927 to 1943 and many became country standards.

The Carter Family consisted of Sara Carter, her husband Alvin 'AP' Carter and his sister-in-law Maybelle Carter. All were born and raised in southwest Virginia and immersed in the tight harmonies of mountain gospel music.

Sara sang lead vocals and played rhythm guitar or autoharp, while Maybelle played lead guitar and sang harmony. AP sang harmony and background vocals but his most significant contribution was as a song collector and arranger. Maybelle's 'Carter scratch' or 'Carter lick' style, which combined lead and rhythm guitar, became a defining feature of their sound.

Their main recording career lasted from 1927 to 1941 and spanned a diverse range of styles, from gospel and blues songs to British folk music and 19th-century parlour songs. Most of these became hits, including 'Wildwood Flower' (1928), 'Keep on the Sunny Side' (1928), 'Wabash Cannonball' (1929), 'John Hardy Was a Desperate Little Man' (1929), and 'Can the Circle Be Unbroken' (1935).

By the mid-1930s they had secured radio contracts, including a lucrative job on a Texas radio station that broadcast over the border into Mexico. At that time they had also added their children into the act: Sara's daughter Janette and Maybelle's girls Helen, June, and Anita.

The Carter Family never crossed over into the mainstream or reaped the level of financial success as Jimmie Rodgers and Gene Autry. But their legacy is profound.

Essential Tracks
- KEEP ON THE SUNNY SIDE
- WILDWOOD FLOWER
- CAN THE CIRCLE BE UNBROKEN

In PBS's *American Experience* documentary series, singer-songwriter Gillian Welch said it was ultimately their prowess as arrangers that would be their enduring legacy. "Sometimes I think they were the best arrangers we've ever seen in roots music and that may in fact be their legacy," said Welch, "that the forms of these songs that we know come to us through them."

> **"THE CARTER FAMILY NEVER CROSSED OVER INTO THE MAINSTREAM, BUT THEIR LEGACY IS PROFOUND"**

BELOW LEFT TO RIGHT: MAYBELLE, SARA AND ALVIN, PICTURED CIRCA 1927.

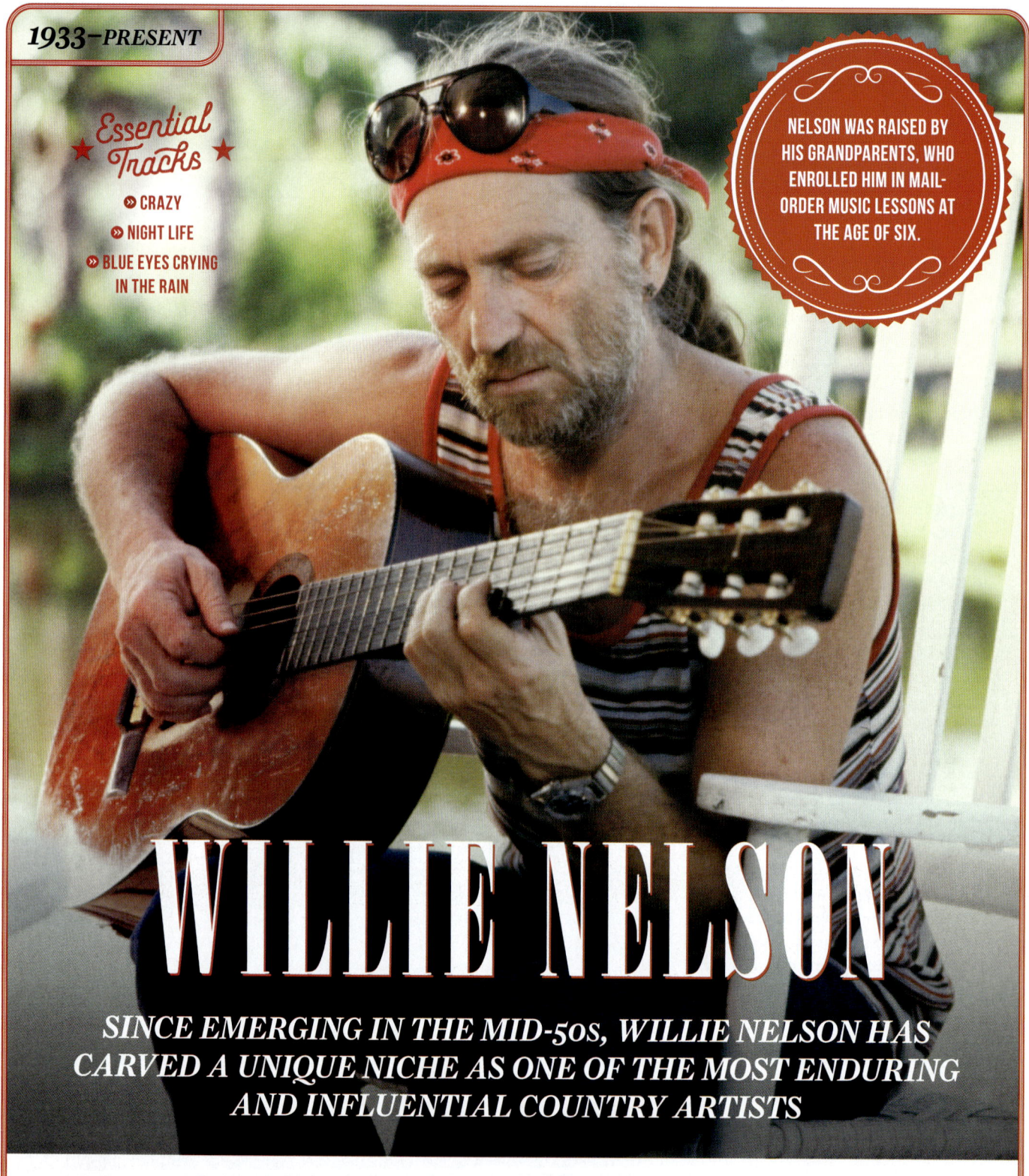

1933–PRESENT

Essential Tracks
- CRAZY
- NIGHT LIFE
- BLUE EYES CRYING IN THE RAIN

NELSON WAS RAISED BY HIS GRANDPARENTS, WHO ENROLLED HIM IN MAIL-ORDER MUSIC LESSONS AT THE AGE OF SIX.

WILLIE NELSON

SINCE EMERGING IN THE MID-50S, WILLIE NELSON HAS CARVED A UNIQUE NICHE AS ONE OF THE MOST ENDURING AND INFLUENTIAL COUNTRY ARTISTS

Across his seven-decade career Willie Nelson has cut right across the grain of country music and created a style that is beguiling and unique. Texas native Nelson started out writing for other artists and a move to Nashville in 1960 sparked a run of hits, such as 'Hello Walls' for Faron Young and 'Crazy' for Patsy Cline.

Minor hits such as 'Bring Me Sunshine' (1969) followed but he railed against the heavily produced Nashville sound. He returned to Texas in 1972 and relaunched himself with an outlaw country sound. The album *Red Headed Stranger* (1975) was a hit and yielded his first No.1 single, 'Blue Eyes Crying in the Rain'.

Pop covers album *Stardust* (1978) sold 4 million copies and in 1982, Nelson's album *Always on My Mind* shot to No.1 on the *Billboard* country chart, as did the song 'Pancho and Lefty', a 1983 duet with Merle Haggard. Three albums with Waylon Jennings fared well, the first yielding the No.1 country hit 'Mammas Don't Let Your Babies Grow Up to Be Cowboys' (1978). A 1985 collaboration as The Highwaymen with Jennings, Kris Kristofferson and Johnny Cash achieved platinum sales.

Nelson's back catalogue is vast, and in 2015, he became the first country artist to receive the Library of Congress Gershwin Prize for Popular Song.

1968–PRESENT

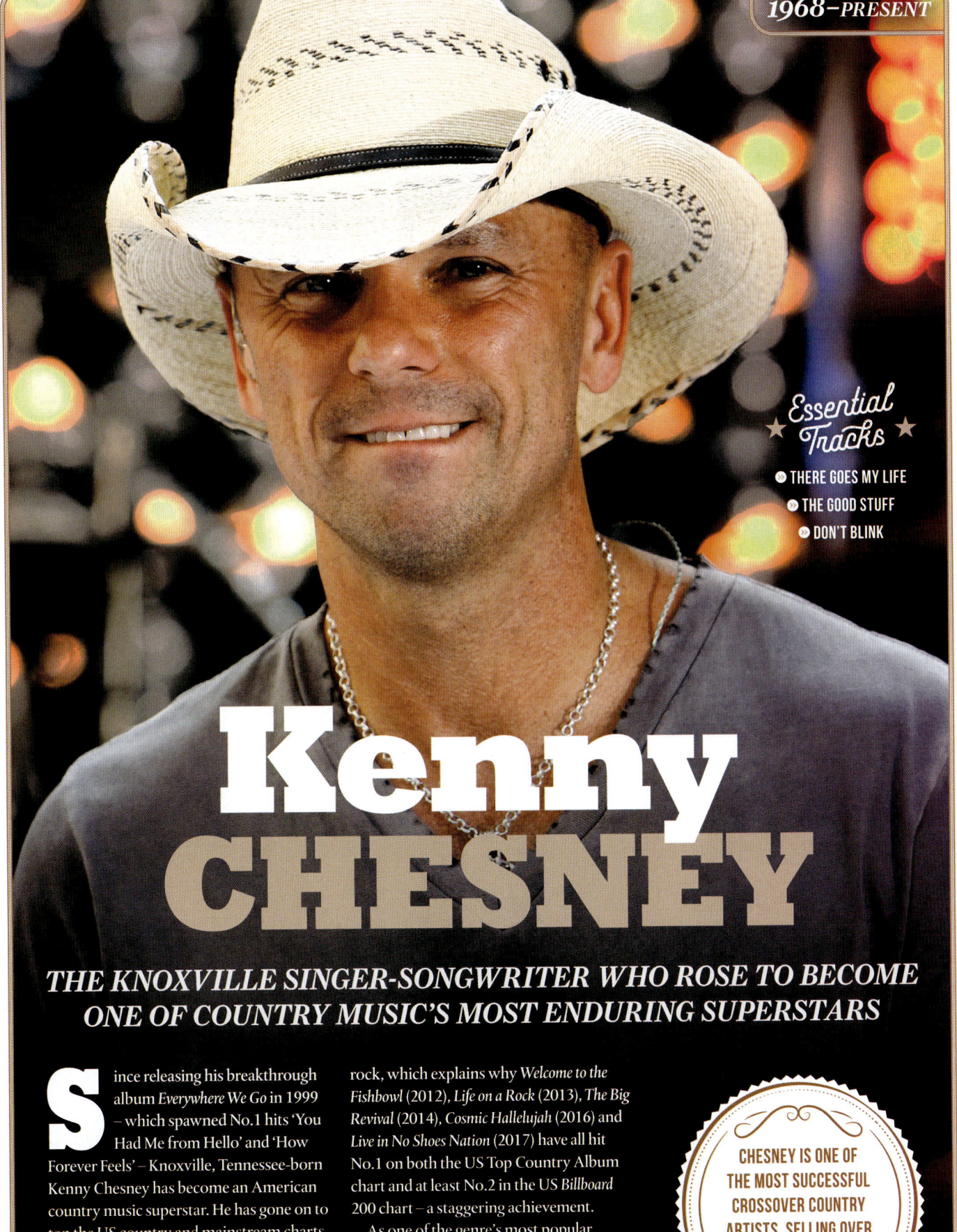

Essential Tracks

- THERE GOES MY LIFE
- THE GOOD STUFF
- DON'T BLINK

Kenny CHESNEY

THE KNOXVILLE SINGER-SONGWRITER WHO ROSE TO BECOME ONE OF COUNTRY MUSIC'S MOST ENDURING SUPERSTARS

Since releasing his breakthrough album *Everywhere We Go* in 1999 – which spawned No.1 hits 'You Had Me from Hello' and 'How Forever Feels' – Knoxville, Tennessee-born Kenny Chesney has become an American country music superstar. He has gone on to top the US country and mainstream charts with albums such as *No Shoes, No Shirt, No Problems* (2002), *When the Sun Goes Down* (2004) and *Lucky Old Sun* (2008).

Stylistically, Chesney spans heartfelt country ballads and strident, mainstream rock, which explains why *Welcome to the Fishbowl* (2012), *Life on a Rock* (2013), *The Big Revival* (2014), *Cosmic Hallelujah* (2016) and *Live in No Shoes Nation* (2017) have all hit No.1 on both the US Top Country Album chart and at least No.2 in the US *Billboard* 200 chart – a staggering achievement.

As one of the genre's most popular touring artists, it is little surprise that both the Academy of Country Music and the Country Music Association have honoured Chesney as Entertainer of the Year on numerous occasions.

CHESNEY IS ONE OF THE MOST SUCCESSFUL CROSSOVER COUNTRY ARTISTS, SELLING OVER 30 MILLION ALBUMS.

Words by Neil Crossley. Image: Getty Images.

1932–2003

JOHNNY CASH

Essential Tracks
- I WALK THE LINE
- HURT
- GOD'S GONNA CUT YOU DOWN

WITH HIS DISTINCTIVE DEEP TONES AND MELANCHOLY, JOHNNY CASH MIGHT JUST BE THE MOST RECOGNISABLE COUNTRY SINGER-SONGWRITER OF ALL TIME

Born 26 February 1932 in Kingsland, Arkansas to a family of poor cotton farmers, J.R. Cash was immersed in the sounds of the rural South from his early childhood, listening to gospel and folk music.

He served in the Air Force in West Germany in the 1950s and learned to play guitar and write songs at the same time, later moving back to the US to marry Vivian Liberto, with whom he settled in Memphis, Tennessee. It was in Memphis where Cash set his sights on a career in music, performing at local events until he auditioned for American disc jockey Sam Phillips and recorded his first tracks including 'Cry! Cry! Cry!' and 'Hey Porter'. His track 'I Walk the Line' reached the number one spot on the country charts in 1957, but Cash was unsatisfied with his recording contract at Sun Records and so he left to join Columbia Records in 1958.

Although he had an outlaw image in the public eye, Cash had only spent brief time in jail for misdemeanours. He chose to wear black because it felt more practical, as it was a colour that was easier to keep clean during live shows, but the dark outfits earned him the nickname of the 'Man in Black'. Cash struggled with drug addiction but eventually sought treatment after encouragement from fellow country singer June Carter, with whom he had toured in the early 1960s. He would later marry the Carter Family star after falling in love with June on tour – it was his second marriage and her third – and he was able to salvage his career with the highly successful recordings of his prison concerts, including *Johnny Cash at San Quentin* (1969).

He achieved more mainstream success with his television series, *The Johnny Cash Show*, but would later face a decline in album sales in the late 1980s. However, he signed a new recording contract with American Recordings and released an album of the same name in 1994, earning him a Grammy. Cash remained a highly revered and well-respected recording artist, activist and global country music superstar until his death in 2003.

> **CASH IS AMONG THE BESTSELLING ARTISTS OF ALL TIME, HAVING SOLD OVER 90 MILLION RECORDS WORLDWIDE.**

LIFE & CAREER

LEFT JOHNNY AND JUNE CARTER CASH WERE MARRIED FROM 1968 UNTIL JUNE'S DEATH IN 2003.

THE IDEA FOR THE MARIACHI-INSPIRED MELODIES ON HIS HIT 'RING OF FIRE' CAME TO CASH IN A DREAM.

» Spontaneous supergroup

Early on in his career at Sun Record Studios, some of the biggest stars at the time made an impromptu recording: Jerry Lee Lewis, Carl Perkins, Elvis Presley and… Johnny Cash. The recording was called 'Million Dollar Quartet' and over the years, extra tracks have been discovered. It's difficult to hear Cash on the recording, but in his 1997 autobiography, he wrote "I was there – I was the first to arrive and the last to leave," continuing, "We all started laughing and cutting up together."

JOHNNY CASH

RIGHT AFTER PERFORMING AT FOLSOM PRISON IN 1966, CASH HAD THIS MUGSHOT TAKEN AS A JOKE WITH THE GUARDS.

Reformer

Throughout his career, Cash used his profile to address social injustice and was interested in penal reform, participating in political hearings on the matter (pictured above with President Nixon). Cash performed in many prisons where he also recorded his performances as albums, with both *Johnny Cash at Folsom Prison* and *Johnny Cash at San Quentin* reaching number one on the *Billboard* country album music chart. His work served to highlight the poor conditions prisoners were being subjected to.

Contemporary covers

In his later years, Cash recorded covers of contemporary rock songs, including 'Personal Jesus' by Depeche Mode, 'One' by U2 and – perhaps most famously – 'Hurt' by Nine Inch Nails. In a 2004 interview with *Alternative Press*, Trent Reznor of Nine Inch Nails explained how he was originally unsure about the Cash cover, but after watching the critically acclaimed, Grammy-winning music video, he admitted "that song isn't mine anymore".

> "CASH USED HIS PROFILE TO ADDRESS SOCIAL INJUSTICE"

Activism

Cash was deeply invested in raising awareness of injustices faced by Native Americans, which really set him apart from most other musicians at the time who shied away from these issues. Cash wrote protest songs about settler violence towards Indigenous peoples – such as on his concept album *Bitter Tears* – despite opposition from his record label at the time who thought they would be viewed as too radical. In recognition of his work, Cash was honoured by the Seneca Nation's Turtle Clan in 1966.

1923–1964

REEVES PLAYED BASEBALL IN THE ST LOUIS CARDINALS MINOR LEAGUE FROM 1944 TO 1947.

Essential Tracks
» HE'LL HAVE TO GO
» MEXICAN JOE
» WELCOME TO MY WORLD

Jim Reeves

'GENTLEMAN JIM' WAS THE BIGGEST MALE STAR TO EMERGE FROM NASHVILLE, WITH SONGS THAT SPOKE TO MILLIONS AROUND THE GLOBE

Galloway, Texas was the birthplace of the man born James Travis Reeves, whose warm, smooth baritone voice and refined style earned him the title of 'Gentleman Jim'. Reeves was the biggest male star to emerge from the Nashville scene and became a pioneer of its sound, blending traditional country music with pop and lush, velvety orchestration. It's a sound that would make Reeves a household name in the US, Europe, India, and South Africa.

Reeves was five when he got his first guitar and he became entranced by country music, particularly Jimmie Rodgers. By his mid-20s he was performing on an amateur basis, but by 1950 he had become a DJ In Shreveport and was hosting the Louisiana Hayride. When Hank Williams failed to show in 1952, Reeves stepped into his place, received rapturous applause, and was snapped up by Abbott Records.

His first single 'Mexican Joe' reached No.1 in 1953. He had four other hits before being signed by RCA in 1955. *Yonder Comes a Sucker* was his first hit with RCA and sparked an astonishing run of 40 hit singles. These included number ones such as 'Four Walls', 'Billy Bayou' and 'He'll Have to Go'. Many crossed over into the mainstream pop market.

Encouraged by his producer Chet Atkins, Reeves started to sing close up to the microphone, crooning in the style of Sinatra and Crosby, singing more quietly and using the lower registers of his voice to bring real depth and intimacy to his vocal sound. This heightened his appeal to pop audiences. Ballads such as 'Adios Amigo' (1962), 'Welcome to My World' (1964), 'I Love You Because' (1964) and 'I Guess I'm Crazy' (1964) became massive Top 5 international hits.

Reeves was at the height of his career when his private plane crashed outside Nashville on 31 July 1964. His death only increased his popularity with posthumous singles such as 'This Is It' (1965), 'Is It Really Over?' (1965), 'Distant Drums' (1966), and 'I Won't Come in While He's There' (1967) all topping the US country chart.

LEFT REEVES PICTURED WITH HIS BAND, THE BLUE BOYS, NAMED AFTER HIS 1958 HIT 'BLUE BOY'.

ABOVE REEVES' CROONER SINGING STYLE HAD MASS APPEAL BEYOND THE COUNTRY CHARTS.

JERRY LEE LEWIS

1935–2022

JERRY LEE LEWIS

Essential Tracks
- CHANTILLY LACE
- TO MAKE LOVE SWEETER FOR YOU
- WHAT'S MADE MILWAUKEE FAMOUS (HAS MADE A LOSER OUT OF ME)

> WHILE COUNTRY FANS LAPPED UP LEWIS'S NEW MUSICAL DIRECTION, HE WAS NEVER TRULY ACCEPTED IN NASHVILLE.

IN THE LATE 60S, THE MAN DUBBED 'THE KILLER' CHANGED COURSE FOR COUNTRY MUSIC AND RARELY LOOKED BACK

While best known as a pioneering rock'n'roller, Jerry Lee Lewis was also one of the greatest country singers of all time. In 1968, the explosive performer known as 'The Killer' made a transition into country music with songs such as 'Another Place, Another Time'. It was a move that reignited his career in the late 60s and through the 70s.

Lewis notched up a stream of No.1 country hits such as 'To Make Love Sweeter for You' (1968), 'There Must Be More to Love Than This' (1970), 'Would You Take Another Chance on Me?' (1971) and 'Me and Bobby McGee' (1971). Between 1969 and 1981, Lewis released 34 Top 20 country singles, which showcased his masterful piano and vocal performances.

Lewis was a natural, having been raised on the music of Jimmy Rodgers, Gene Autrey and Hank Williams. Sadly, he was too ill to attend his induction by Hank Williams Jnr into the Country Music Hall of fame on 16 October 2022, just twelve days before his death at the age of 87.

1936–PRESENT

KRISTOFFERSON WAS DUE TO BEGIN TEACHING ENGLISH AT WEST POINT BEFORE HE HEADED TO NASHVILLE.

Essential Tracks
- ME AND BOBBY MCGEE
- HELP ME MAKE IT THROUGH THE NIGHT
- SUNDAY MORNIN' COMIN' DOWN

KRIS KRISTOFFERSON

A UNIQUELY GIFTED SINGER, SONGWRITER AND ACTOR WHO HAS CRAFTED A STRING OF ICONIC COUNTRY SONGS

Kris Kristofferson had been a US Army captain, a helicopter pilot and a Rhodes scholar before heading for Nashville in 1965. He went on to create a catalogue of timeless and majestic songs.

Texas-born Kristofferson struggled in Nashville until Roger Miller's cover of his song 'Me and Bobby McGee' (1969) reached the country Top 20. Two No.1 hits followed in 1970: Ray Price's 'For the Good Times' and Johnny Cash's 'Sunday Mornin' Comin' Down'.

Kristofferson's 1970 debut solo album was a failure, yet covers of his songs by other artists filled the charts, such as Sammi Smith's version of 'Help Me Make It Through the Night' (1970).

His major breakthrough came when Janis Joplin's version of 'Me and Bobby McGee' hit topped the pop charts. Kristofferson scored his own No.1 country hit with 'Why Me' (1973) and had successful 70s albums with his then wife Rita Coolidge. By the mid-70s, he was carving a successful career as a film actor.

In 1985, he teamed up with Johnny Cash, Willie Nelson and Waylon Jennings to form the supergroup The Highwaymen, releasing their hugely successful outlaw country debut, *Highwayman*.

In 2004, Kristofferson was inducted into the Country Music Hall of Fame. He remains a unique talent, a renaissance man of the country music scene.

1934–2020

CHARLEY PRIDE

CHARLEY PRIDE PAVED THE WAY FOR OTHER BLACK COUNTRY MUSICIANS, ACHIEVING 30 CHART-TOPPING HITS

A true multi-hyphenate, Charley Pride was not only a gifted musician, but also a professional baseball player. Pride had a humble upbringing; his parents were sharecroppers. This spurred him on to want to forge a better future for himself and his family, and at just 14 years old, he taught himself how to play guitar. But he was also a talented sportsman, and Pride began playing for the Memphis Red Sox of the Negro American League when he was around 18 (his brother, Mack, also played for the Red Sox). Pride attempted to break into music by approaching Sun Studios – the same place Elvis Presley was discovered – but had little success. It wasn't until 1960, when he moved to Montana to play baseball, that he began singing before each game and in local bars.

Five years later, he moved to Nashville and 'Cowboy' Jack Clement became his manager. Initially, Clement thought he might find success as a novelty act, but Pride persevered and in 1966, he signed with RCA Victor, releasing his debut album *Country Charley Pride*. With his distinctive baritone voice and warm, crooning lyrics, he enjoyed chart success throughout his career, which was remarkable given the rampant racism in the country music industry and more broadly across the nation at the time. However, it should be noted that his label chose not to release publicity photos of Pride to accompany his first few songs for radio.

Pride reached number one in the US country chart with his track 'All I Have to Offer You (Is Me)' in 1969, and released 12 further number one hits over the next few years, including 'Kiss an Angel Good Mornin'' in 1971. He also won the 1973 Grammy Award for Best Male Country Vocal Performance. Despite being the label's bestselling performer in the previous decade, RCA dropped Pride in 1985 after deciding to promote younger country-pop artists. He continued with his career, however, and won a lifetime achievement award at the 2017 Grammys. Pride passed away in December 2020 from complications arising due to Covid-19, but his trailblazing legacy lives on.

PRIDE WAS INDUCTED INTO THE COUNTRY MUSIC HALL OF FAME IN 2000.

LEFT PRIDE IS REGARDED AS COUNTRY MUSIC'S FIRST BLACK SUPERSTAR.

RIGHT PERFORMING TO A SOLD-OUT CROWD AT MADISON SQUARE GARDEN'S FELT FORUM IN 1975.

CHARLEY PRIDE

Essential Tracks

» KISS AN ANGEL GOOD MORNIN'
» IS ANYBODY GOIN' TO SAN ANTONE
» MOUNTAIN OF LOVE

ALABAMA

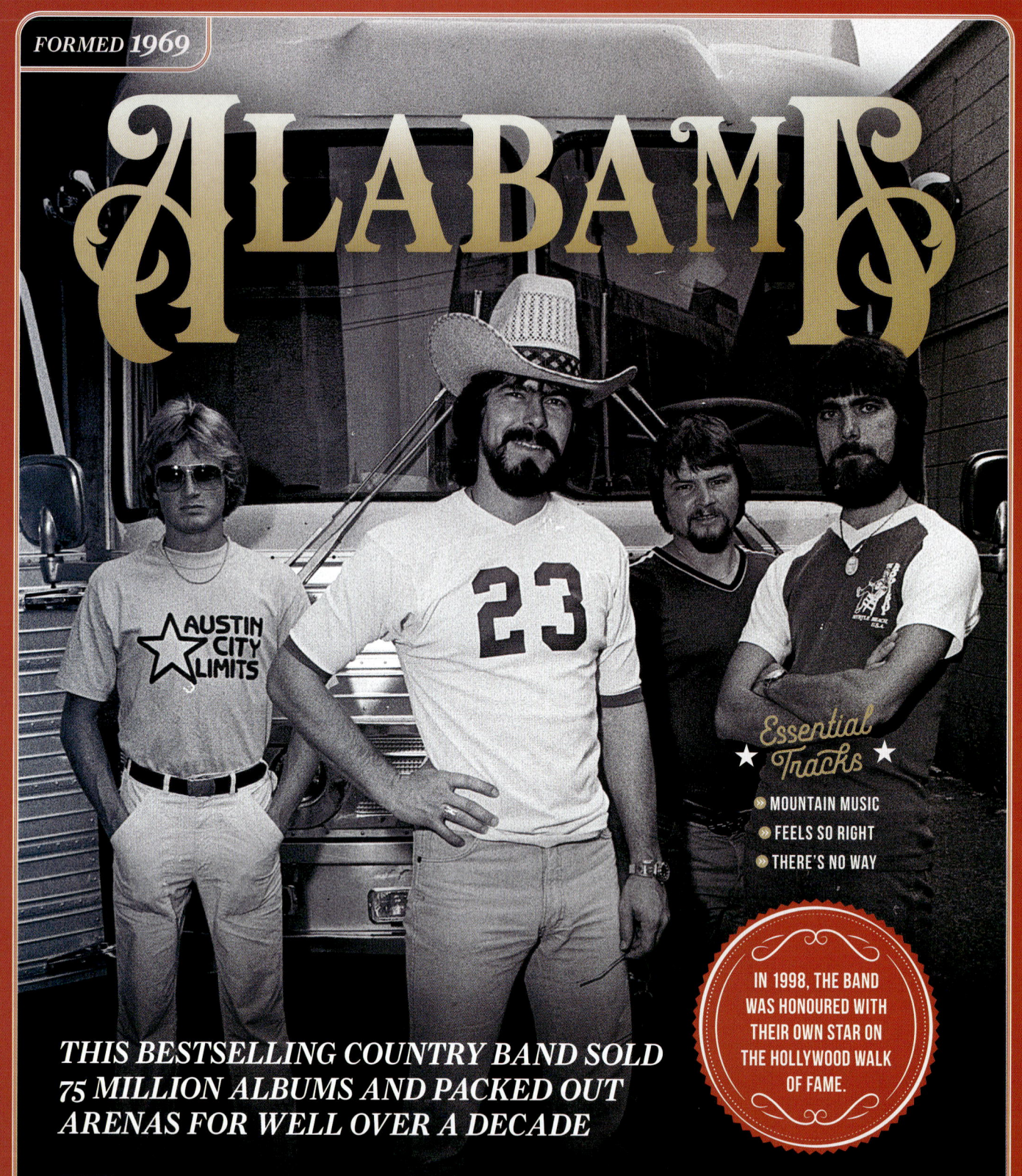

FORMED 1969

ALABAMA

Essential Tracks
- MOUNTAIN MUSIC
- FEELS SO RIGHT
- THERE'S NO WAY

IN 1998, THE BAND WAS HONOURED WITH THEIR OWN STAR ON THE HOLLYWOOD WALK OF FAME.

THIS BESTSELLING COUNTRY BAND SOLD 75 MILLION ALBUMS AND PACKED OUT ARENAS FOR WELL OVER A DECADE

Rock-inspired four-piece Alabama were the most popular country band of the 80s, with hits such as 'Mountain Music' and 'My Home's in Alabama'. Between 1980 and 1993, the band had over 30 No.1 singles on the *Billboard* country chart and sold 75 million albums.

Alabama was formed by three cousins: Randy Owen (lead vocal, guitar), Jeff Cook (lead guitar, vocals), and Teddy Gentry (bass), plus Mark Herndon (drums). They played sleek country-rock, combining the Bakersfield sound with bluegrass and smooth Nashville pop.

Their success was rapid. Between 1980 and 1982, Alabama notched up eight No.1 singles on the US country chart, including trademark numbers such as 'Tennessee River' and 'Feels So Right'. Many of their singles and platinum-selling albums also became pop crossover hits.

By the mid-90s, the band's popularity had declined. They originally decided to disband in 2004 after the American Farewell Tour, but reunited in 2010. Cook died in 2022, five years after being diagnosed with Parkinson's disease.

Part of Alabama's legacy is that they helped to elevate the status of bands in country music from backing musicians to artists in their own right. Their music also significantly broadened country's appeal to mainstream audiences.

1946–PRESENT

DUBBED THE QUEEN OF COUNTRY-ROCK, LINDA RONSTADT'S VERSATILITY AND VOCAL VIRTUOSITY ENSURED HER SUPERSTAR STATUS

LINDA RONSTADT

Essential Tracks
- BLUE BAYOU
- DESPERADO
- YOU'RE NO GOOD

Few country artists have spanned such a diverse range of genres as Linda Ronstadt, who was at the forefront of country-rock in the 70s. She is best known for her astute choice of songs that best suit her astonishingly rich and powerful voice, always putting her own unique stamp on them. It's a talent that would catapult her to mainstream stardom.

Ronstadt broke through with her 1974 solo album *Heart Like a Wheel*, which reached No.1 and sold over 2 million copies. The albums *Prisoner in Disguise* (1975) and *Hasten Down the Wind* (1976) were similarly successful. She moved into contemporary rock and pop in the early 80s but returned to her country roots in 1987, recording the *Trio* album with Dolly Parton and Emmylou Harris.

In the same year, she explored her Mexican heritage with a bestselling album of Mexican folk songs called *Canciones de Mi Padre*. She was drawn back to country-rock in 1995 for the album *Feels Like Home*.

Over the years, Ronstadt has collaborated with artists from a vast range of genres, such as The Chieftains on the 2010 album *San Patricio*. In 2013, Ronstadt revealed she has Parkinson's disease, which has prevented her from singing. Having sold more than 100 million albums worldwide, Ronstadt has been a hugely influential force in the music industry.

RONSTADT'S SONG 'LONG, LONG TIME' HAD A RESURGENCE IN 2023 AFTER FEATURING IN HBO'S THE LAST OF US.

1937–2016

MERLE HAGGARD

A GIANT OF COUNTRY MUSIC WHO DEFINED THE BAKERSFIELD SOUND AND WAS KNOWN AS THE 'POET OF THE COMMON MAN'

Few country artists have been as popular and widely admired as Merle Haggard. Between the 1960s and 1980s the singer-songwriter topped the US country charts a staggering 38 times with songs that resonated with working-class people.

Born in Oildale, California to Oklahoman migrant worker parents, Haggard left home at 14 and drifted into petty crime, spending his 21st birthday in the state prison at San Quentin, convicted for burglary. After being paroled in 1960, he resolved to be a country singer, like his role models Lefty Frizzell and Jimmie Rodgers.

He began singing with Buck Owens' ex-wife, Bonnie, formed a band, The Strangers, and signed with Capitol Records. He scored his first No.1 hit on the *Billboard* country chart with 'I'm a Lonesome Fugitive', written by Liz and Casey Anderson.

By the late 60s, Haggard was a household name, guesting on TV shows, thanks to songs such as 'Sing Me Back Home'. Some of his finest songs, such as 'Branded Man' and 'Mama Tried', were inspired by his time in prison.

He spearheaded the twangy Bakersfield sound, which was edgier than its Nashville counterpart.

In 1969, he wrote 'Okie from Muskogee', an anti-hippy song, which reached No.1 in the US country charts and crossed into the mainstream. He released 'The Fightin' Side of Me' in 1970, a jingoistic response to the anti-Vietnam movement. That same year, he released *Same Train, Different Time*, an album of songs associated with Jimmie Rodgers, and recorded 'Workin' Man Blues', an anthem for the overworked and underpaid, which shot to the top of the US Hot Country Songs chart.

Haggard's life was punctuated by bouts of heavy drinking, as detailed in songs such as 'I Think I'll Just Stay Here and Drink' (1980). By then he would select only those projects that really appealed such as the million-selling album *Pancho and Lefty*, with Willie Nelson in 1983.

Haggard kept a low profile in the 90s but returned in the Noughties with 2001's *Roots, Volume 1*, which paid tribute to influences such as Hank Williams.

By then he was a living legend and would influence the country stars of the new millennium such as The Chicks. When asked by journalist Paul Hemphill how he would like to be remembered, he replied: "As a writer, somebody who did some living and wrote songs about what he knew. That's all."

THE WRITERS OF 'I'M A LONESOME FUGITIVE' HAD NO IDEA THAT HAGGARD WAS A FORMER PRISONER.

> "'WORKIN' MAN BLUES' WAS AN ANTHEM FOR THE OVERWORKED AND UNDERPAID"

Essential Tracks

- SING ME BACK HOME
- MAMA TRIED
- OKIE FROM MUSKOGEE

1946–PRESENT

Dolly Parton

THE QUEEN OF COUNTRY, DOLLY PARTON HAS HAD A SEISMIC EFFECT, NOT ONLY ON THE GENRE, BUT ACROSS POP CULTURE

52 COUNTRY MUSIC ICONS

DOLLY PARTON

Dolly Parton has made the rare step into true legend status through her astonishing musical legacy, her charm, and her forays into pop culture. Her songwriting prowess created some of the most successful songs of all time: including the timeless 'Jolene' and 'I Will Always Love You', both of which Parton wrote in a single night. Her career paved the way for many female country artists to come.

Parton began her musical career primarily performing duets in country showcase TV programme *The Porter Wagoner Show*. It was during this time she was signed to RCA Records, initially as a duet partner for Wagoner and eventually surpassing him as a solo artist. Parton's solo success began in earnest in the mid-1970s with a string of chart hits including 'Coat of Many Colors' – an enduring song that inspired a children's book and a film.

Parton pursued crossover pop success through the 1980s, notably releasing '9 to 5' alongside her starring role in the film of the same name. In this time, she secured her dominance outside of the country genre and earned multiple high-profile accolades, including nominations for EGOT status. Although she was becoming a household name, Parton did shift away from country music to focus on crossover stardom and her film, theatre and business careers. It wasn't until the late 90s that she returned to her roots, releasing a series of critically acclaimed bluegrass albums.

In addition to her prolific songwriting abilities, Parton is also a skilled multi-instrumentalist, playing an eclectic mix from the banjo to the autoharp. While her musical talent is undeniable, she has downplayed her gifts by modestly claiming that she does not play any of them particularly well, she just "really sells it". Her unmistakable brand, encompassing an iconic look, outrageous outfits and her trademark wit, has cemented Parton as a globally adored figure.

LEFT THE TRUE STORY BEHIND PARTON'S 'COAT OF MANY COLORS' WAS TURNED INTO A 2015 FILM BASED ON HER CHILDHOOD.

RIGHT ON STAGE AT GLASTONBURY IN 2014, WHEN PARTON PLAYED THE LEGENDS SLOT.

SHE ONCE ENTERED A DRAG 'DOLLY PARTON LOOKALIKE' CONTEST... AND LOST!

Essential Tracks
- JOLENE
- ISLANDS IN THE STREAM
- JUST BECAUSE I'M A WOMAN

COUNTRY MUSIC ICONS 53

LIFE & CAREER

» Award winner

Parton's career has been studded by a near-historic number of award nominations. Among the many trophies and accolades, she has received some of the industry's highest honours. As of June 2024, this includes being one of only eight women ever to be awarded the CMA's Entertainer of the Year Award in 1978 (alongside her ten awards across 45 nominations by the organisation). In 2011, Parton was awarded a Lifetime Achievement Award for her "contributions of outstanding artistic significance" by the Grammys.

> **"PARTON'S CAREER HAS BEEN STUDDED BY A NEAR-HISTORIC NUMBER OF AWARD NOMINATIONS"**

» National treasure

Parton is officially a cornerstone of American culture. She was presented with the National Medal of Arts and later given the Living Legend Medal by the Library of Congress in recognition of her enormous contributions to the American cultural landscape. Her song 'Coat of Many Colors' was also entered into the Library of Congress's National Recording Registry. She has even been offered the highest civilian honour of a Presidential Medal of Freedom twice, but she turned it down – first because her husband was ill, and second due to the Covid pandemic.

» Hall of famer

Parton has been inducted into many halls of fame: including three entries in the Grammy Hall of Fame (once each for 'I Will Always Love You', 'Jolene' and 'Coat of Many Colors'). She is in two songwriting-specific halls of fame, and genre-specific halls of fame (including Gospel and Rock and Roll). Perhaps her most significant induction is to the Country Music Hall of Fame in 1999, one of the genre's highest honours.

DOLLY PARTON

> PARTON OWNS THE TENNESSEE THEME PARK DOLLYWOOD, COMPLETE WITH A WATER PARK AND RENOWNED LIVE SHOWS.

⬆ Generous spirit

Parton's philanthropic work has been a consistent part of her career. She founded the Dollywood Foundation, which funds a number of charitable projects across a wide range of causes. This includes financial support for Covid-19 vaccines, her Imagination Library book-gifting charity, animal conservation, disaster relief funding, and medical causes. She has also been credited with providing economic uplift to her home state through the development of jobs – both across her philanthropic and commercial work.

1899–1992

Essential Tracks
- PAN AMERICAN BLUES
- KANSAS CITY BLUES
- FOX CHASE

> BAILEY LEARNED THE HARMONICA WHILE BEDRIDDEN WITH POLIO AT THE AGE OF THREE, AS HE COULD ONLY MOVE HIS HEAD AND ARMS.

DEFORD BAILEY

AN INFLUENTIAL HARMONICA PLAYER, PIONEER MEMBER OF THE GRAND OLE OPRY AND COUNTRY'S FIRST AFRICAN-AMERICAN STAR

"There is a gulf of Biblical proportions between the amount of influence American Black music has had on country & western and the number of Black performers actually involved in country," wrote Eugene Chadbourne of *AllMusic* in his biography of DeFord Bailey, an influential harmonica player in country and blues music.

Bailey, whose growth was severely stunted by polio, was country music's first African-American star. In 1925, he was invited to play a radio show called WSN Barn Dance, which two years later changed its name to the Grand Ole Opry.

Bailey attracted a large audience, which was bolstered further by appearances with stars such as Roy Acuff and Bill Monroe. Even so, he faced racism and the indignities of segregation throughout his working life.

His radio career came to an abrupt halt in 1941 following a dispute over music licensing. Bailey was fired and left the music profession, although he did occasionally make guest appearances at the Opry.

JOHN DENVER

1943–1997

Essential Tracks
- TAKE ME HOME, COUNTRY ROADS
- SUNSHINE ON MY SHOULDERS
- DANNIE'S SONG

A COUNTRY-FOLK SINGER-SONGWRITER WHO BECAME ONE OF THE BIGGEST STARS OF THE 70s

IN 1976, DENVER CAMPAIGNED FOR FUTURE PRESIDENT JIMMY CARTER, WHO BECAME A CLOSE FRIEND AND ALLY.

John Denver

Born Henry John Deutschendorf Jr, the singer-songwriter who would become known as John Denver emerged from the 60s folk revival to become one of the most beloved entertainers of his generation.

Denver gained a foothold in the industry when his song 'Leaving on a Jet Plane' was a No.2 hit for Peter, Paul and Mary in February 1970.

His breakthrough came with second album *Poems, Prayers and Promises* (1971) and the single 'Take Me Home, Country Roads', a No.2 hit on the *Billboard* charts. A stream of hits followed such as 'Sunshine on My Shoulders' (1973), 'Annie's Song' (1974) and 'Thank God I'm a Country Boy' (1974).

Melodic hooks pervaded Denver's breezy country-folk sound and with his long blonde hair, easy smile and wire-rimmed granny glasses, he cut a dynamic yet amiable figure. In 1973, he landed his own weekly music and variety TV series on the BBC, while his best-of compilation album in 1974 remained on the charts for over two years.

Denver's popularity waned in the 80s and he focused on humanitarian work. He died at the age of 53 when the light aircraft he was piloting crashed in Monterey Bay, California.

1919–2012

Essential Tracks

- IT WASN'T GOD WHO MADE HONKY TONK ANGELS
- HEARTBREAK USA
- I HEARD THE JUKEBOX PLAYING

WELLS WAS THE FIRST FEMALE SOLO ARTIST TO TOP THE US COUNTRY CHART.

KITTY WELLS

DUBBED THE QUEEN OF COUNTRY MUSIC, KITTY WELLS PAVED THE WAY FOR SOLO FEMALE ARTISTS IN NASHVILLE

One of the few country stars to have actually been born in Nashville, Kitty Wells broke down barriers for women, paving the way for artists such as Patsy Cline, Tammy Wynette and Loretta Lynn. During the 1950s she racked up a welter of Top 10 hits and her gospel-infused vocals and plaintive vocal delivery resonated with country audiences.

Born Ellen Muriel Deason in Nashville, Tennessee, she came from a musical family. She began performing with her two sisters and cousins in the Deason Sisters. In 1937, she married singer Johnnie Wright, who gave Wells her stage name, taken from a Pickard Family song.

In 1949, Wells recorded some gospel tracks that yielded little interest. But her fortunes changed dramatically in 1952 when an executive at Decca Records approached Wells to record 'It Wasn't God Who Made Honky Tonk Angels'.

The track was an 'answer song' to Hank Thompson's hit 'The Wild Side of Life'. Wells's song, written by JD Miller, argued that it was not women's frailties that were responsible for them falling on hard times but uncaring, deceitful men.

It was a controversial viewpoint in the South but audiences couldn't get enough of it. The song shot to No.1 in the US national country charts, sold more than 800,000 copies in its initial release and crossed over to *Billboard*'s pop chart, hitting No.27.

More hits followed, such as 'Paying for That Back Street Affair', 'Heartbreak USA' and 'Broken Marriage Vows'. These were emotionally wrought honky-tonk ballads that spoke of sin and redemption. By the end of the Fifties, Wells had clocked up more than 30 Top 10 hits.

But after her 1962 song 'Will Your Lawyer Talk to God', the run of hits ceased, although Wells' stalwart fans remained loyal, regularly tuning into her syndicated television programme.

Wells had a significant influence on other female artists, inspiring the likes of Emmylou Harris, Pam Tillis, Patty Loveless and Lee Ann Womack to name a few. In 1976, she was elected to the Country Music Hall of Fame and at the Grammy ceremony and in 1991, Wells received a lifetime achievement award. She was the first woman in country music to be honoured in this way.

> **BY THE END OF THE 1950s, WELLS HAD CLOCKED UP MORE THAN 30 TOP 10 HITS**

RIGHT WELLS WITH HER HUSBAND JOHNNIE WRIGHT AND THE TENNESSEE HILLBILLIES.

FAR RIGHT A PORTRAIT OF WELLS IN 1991 WITH HER GRAMMY LIFETIME ACHIEVEMENT AWARD.

THE LOUVIN BROTHERS

ACTIVE 1940–1963

Essential Tracks
- I DON'T BELIEVE YOU'VE MET MY BABY
- YOU'RE RUNNING WILD
- HOPING THAT YOU'RE HOPING

THE LOUVINS' DEBUT SINGLE 'THE FAMILY WHO PRAYS' BECAME A GOSPEL STANDARD.

THE LOUVIN BROTHERS

THE MOST INFLUENTIAL HARMONY DUO IN THE HISTORY OF COUNTRY MUSIC LEFT A RICH, ENDURING LEGACY

Like many first-generation country artists, gospel music was a major influence on the music of Ira and Charlie Louvin (né Loudermilk), a country, bluegrass and gospel duo who popularised the close harmony vocal style that would influence artists such as the Everly Brothers, Gram Parsons, Emmylou Harris, The Byrds, Marty Stuart and Gillian Welch.

Ira and Charlie scored a string of hit singles in the late 50s and early 60s, such as 'When I Stop Dreaming' (1955), 'I Don't Believe You've Met My Baby' (1955), 'Cash on the Barrelhead' (1956) and 'My Baby's Gone' (1960).

The Louvin Brothers' high, lonesome harmonies and Ira's sublime mandolin work created a powerfully emotive sound. Their songs spanned secular themes alongside those influenced by their Baptist faith that focused on sin and redemption.

The duo split in 1963, partly due to Ira's drinking and his ferocious temper. But their traditional Appalachian country music sound would inspire legions of country and country rock artists who followed in their wake.

Words by Neil Crossley. Image: Getty Images.

60 COUNTRY MUSIC ICONS

BRAD PAISLEY

1972–PRESENT

PAISLEY HAS WRITTEN TWO BOOKS: *JUG FISHING...* (2003) AND HIS AUTOBIOGRAPHY *DIARY OF A PLAYER* (2011).

Essential Tracks

- WELCOME TO THE FUTURE
- WITHOUT A FIGHT (WITH DEMI LOVATO)
- SAME HERE (WITH UKRAINIAN PRESIDENT VOLODYMYR ZELENSKY)

BRAD PAISLEY

A STAR FOR 30 YEARS AND COUNTING, MR PAISLEY HAS EVEN COLLABORATED WITH WORLD LEADERS

Born and raised in Glen Dale, West Virginia, Brad Daisley fell in love with country music when his grandfather gave him his first guitar at eight years old. He wrote his first song, 'Born on Christmas Day', at the age of 13, and by the time he graduated high school he was a regular performer on the famous country radio show, *Jamboree USA*. After college he signed a record deal and scored a No.1 hit in 1999 with 'He Didn't Have to Be'. Two years later, he was a platinum-selling artist: remarkably, he has managed to maintain his momentum in the almost quarter-century since then, amassing a shelfload of awards for his songs and videos.

In 2024, Paisley released his 13th studio album, having raised eyebrows worldwide the year before by releasing a single called 'Same Here' that featured the Ukrainian President Volodymyr Zelensky, although that beleaguered head of state appears in conversation rather than singing or playing an instrument.

COUNTRY MUSIC ICONS

1955–PRESENT

REBA McENTIRE

THIS QUEEN OF COUNTRY MUSIC BECAME ONE OF THE GENRE'S MOST SUCCESSFUL ARTISTS AND ALSO CREATED A MUSIC BUSINESS EMPIRE

Born and raised in Oklahoma, Reba McEntire was the most successful country star of her generation, selling over 75 million records and having 100 singles in the *Billboard* Hot Country Songs, 25 of which reached No.1.

McEntire grew up on a sprawling 8,000-acre cattle ranch and began performing with her brother and sister in the Singing McEntires. She was signed to Mercury Records after being spotted singing the national anthem at the National Finals Rodeo in Oklahoma City.

McEntire has a powerful, emotive voice, with a natural down-home feel. In 1979, her rendition of Patsy Cline's 'Sweet Dreams' reached the Top 20 and she went on to score No.1s with 'Can't Even Get the Blues' (1982) and 'You're the First Time I've Thought About Leaving' (1983).

Her raw, rootsy covers album *My Kind of Country* (1984) yielded the No.1 hits 'How Blue' and 'Somebody Should Leave' and she joined the cast of the Grand Ole Opry in 1986.

In 1987, McEntire moved to Nashville and began building substantial business enterprises. She adopted a smoother sound for her 1988 album, *Reba*, which featured elements of pop and R&B. Two years on, in the fall of 1990, the soaring, heartfelt track 'You Lie', from her 17th album *Rumour Has It*, dominated the airwaves.

But McEntire faced tragedy in March 1991 when seven members of her band and her road manager were killed when their plane hit a mountain during take-off from San Diego. Haunted by this disaster, McEntire took an extended break from touring and recording. In October that year, she released the album *For My Broken Heart*, in memory of her friends who had died.

By the new millennium McEntire was expanding into new areas. In 2001, she was critically lauded when she starred in the Broadway revival of *Annie Get Your Gun* and that same year, she starred in the TV

> "MCENTIRE HAS A POWERFUL, EMOTIVE VOICE, WITH A NATURAL DOWN-HOME FEEL

LEFT MCENTIRE STARRED AS ANNIE OAKLEY IN THE 1995 TV MINISERIES *BUFFALO GIRLS*.

62 COUNTRY MUSIC ICONS

REBA MCENTIRE

BELOW
MCENTIRE IS A REGULAR HOST OF THE ACADEMY OF COUNTRY MUSIC AWARDS.

MCENTIRE'S FILM-ACTING CAREER BEGAN IN 1990 WITH A ROLE IN THE CULT COMEDY HORROR *TREMORS*.

comedy *Reba*, a popular show that ran for six seasons. In 2007, she scored her first No.1 on the album charts with *Reba: Duets*, featuring Justin Timberlake and Carole King among others. In 2010, 'Turn On the Radio' from her album *All the Women I Am* followed 2009 single 'Consider Me Gone' by topping *Billboard*'s Hot Country Songs chart.

McEntire was inducted into the Country Music Hall of Fame in 2011 and, in 2018, received a Kennedy Center Honor. When once asked about the key to succeeding as a female country artist, she succinctly replied: "Be different, stand out and work your butt off."

Essential Tracks
» YOU LIE
» SOMEBODY SHOULD LEAVE
» FANCY

COUNTRY MUSIC ICONS 63

1962–PRESENT

garth brooks

GARTH BROOKS HAS ENJOYED WIDESPREAD APPEAL AS AN ARTIST UNAFRAID TO BLEND COUNTRY WITH POP AND ROCK

Brooks was named the AMAs' Artist of the 90s and iHeartRadio's Artist of the Decade in 2019.

Garth Brooks was born on 7 February 1962 in Tulsa, Oklahoma, into a musical family: his mother, Colleen McElroy Carroll was a country artist in the 1950s. Despite this, a young Brooks was more interested in sports, and was awarded a track and field scholarship to study at Oklahoma State University, where he graduated in 1984 with an MBA in advertising.

In 1985, Brooks moved to Nashville… for less than 24 hours. He quickly decided to return to Oklahoma after realising Music City wouldn't make him a star overnight. He didn't give up on Nashville, though. The following year, Brooks married his first wife, Sandy Mahl, who he has credited for supporting him during his second shot in the city. The couple moved back there in 1987 and he later signed a deal with Capitol Records.

Brooks' self-titled debut album was released in 1989, and he played shows to support it with his college friend, Ty England, establishing a charismatic live on-stage persona for the duo. He then released the incredibly successful album *No Fences* in 1990, which included the iconic track 'Friends in Low Places' and was number one in the *Billboard* country albums chart for an unbelievable 23 weeks. He has sometimes experimented with his sound and even released a festive album called *Beyond the Season* in 1992, which was the most successful Christmas album that year.

After feeling torn between his family life and his career, Brooks decided to take a break from music, announcing his retirement in October 2000. In the lead-up to his initial retirement, he released his eighth album, *Scarecrow*, in November 2001, which topped the *Billboard* 200 chart. He married fellow country musician, Trisha Yearwood, in 2005, and continued to make a few live performance appearances.

He suspended his retirement in 2009 with his first Las Vegas residency, and several years later released his comeback album, 2014's *Man Against Machine*, and embarked on a huge 390-show world tour. Since then, he has continued to tour, performed a second sold-out Vegas residency, and has released new music, so clearly there's more to come from Brooks.

★ Essential Tracks ★
- IF TOMORROW NEVER COMES
- FRIENDS IN LOW PLACES
- THE DANCE

> **BROOKS MOVED TO NASHVILLE… FOR LESS THAN 24 HOURS**

GARTH BROOKS

ABOVE BROOKS SANG 'AMAZING GRACE' AT PRESIDENT BIDEN'S INAUGURATION IN 2021.

LIFE & CAREER

» Brooks the businessman

Not only is he an incredibly successful recording artist, he's a businessman, too: Brooks set up his record label, Pearl Records, in 2005 after leaving Capitol Records. Additionally, he founded an online music store in 2014 called GhostTunes, on which he released his own music as well as music from other artists. The business was acquired by Amazon Music in 2017.

According to the RIAA, Brooks is the bestselling solo album artist in the US, and second only to The Beatles overall.

> **BROOKS HAS CONTINUED TO TOUR, PERFORMED A SECOND SOLD-OUT VEGAS RESIDENCY, AND HAS RELEASED NEW MUSIC**

Inclusive attitude

Brooks is a proud advocate for the LGBTQ+ community, encouraged by his late half-sister, Betsy Smittle, who identified as a lesbian. Brooks' gospel and country song 'We Shall Be Free', released in 1992, included the lyrics "When we're free to love anyone we choose" as a nod to LGBTQ+ rights. The following year, he was honoured at the GLAAD Media Awards for the song and his advocacy.

Would-be sportsman

Brooks had a brief baseball career, signing with the San Diego Padres, the New York Mets and the Kansas City Royals, but could never achieve the required performance for regular appearances in the teams. His love for sport led him to establish the Teammates for Kids Foundation in 1999, consisting of the baseball Touch 'Em All Foundation, hockey's Top Shelf and American football's Touchdown. The foundation raises money for children in need.

Secret rock persona

In 1999, Brooks had a brief stint as a rock'n'roll musician under the pseudonym Chris Gaines. Chris was a character in his shelved film *The Lamb*, which Brooks intended to be a thriller focusing on a superfan-centred murder mystery storyline. With little context, he released an album in the run-up to the film entitled *Garth Brooks in… the Life of Chris Gaines*, much to the confusion of his fans and critics alike.

TOBY KEITH

1961–2024

Essential Tracks
- RED SOLO CUP
- AS GOOD AS I ONCE WAS
- SHOULD'VE BEEN A COWBOY

TOBY KEITH

A POPULAR AND OUTSPOKEN COUNTRY SINGER-SONGWRITER WHOSE RUGGED STYLE RESONATED WITH THE HEARTLAND OF AMERICA

Country fans were in mourning in February 2024 following the death of Toby Keith, a major country music star who sold over 40 million albums.

Oklahoma-born Keith released his debut album in 1993 and its lead single, 'Should've Been a Cowboy', shot to No.1. The albums *Boomtown* (1995) and *Blue Moon* (1996) were also massive hits. In 2002, Keith responded to the 9/11 attacks with 'Courtesy of the Red, White and Blue', from the album *Unleashed*, which debuted at the top of the US country and pop charts. The single resonated with patriotic fans, but others saw it as aggressively jingoistic. The album also produced the No.1 single 'Who's Your Daddy?' and 'Beer for My Horses', a duet with Willie Nelson.

Sales dipped in the 2010s, although his output remained prolific. The acclaimed 2011 album *Clancy's Tavern* included the hit single 'Red Solo Cup'.

Flags in Oklahoma were ordered to be flown at half-mast following his passing, "as a show of respect and mourning for the loss of American music legend Toby Keith".

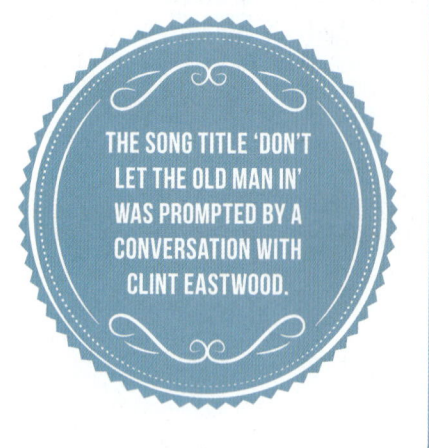

THE SONG TITLE 'DON'T LET THE OLD MAN IN' WAS PROMPTED BY A CONVERSATION WITH CLINT EASTWOOD.

68 COUNTRY MUSIC ICONS

JOHNNY RODRIGUEZ

JOHNNY RODRIGUEZ

1951–PRESENT

Essential Tracks
- RIDIN' MY THUMB TO MEXICO
- YOU ALWAYS COME BACK (TO HURTING ME)
- THAT'S THE WAY LOVE GOES

BY 1975, RODRIGUEZ WAS CONSIDERED A MEMBER OF THE OUTLAW COUNTRY MARKET.

THIS PROLIFIC 70S HITMAKER WAS THE FIRST HISPANIC AMERICAN TO BECOME A COUNTRY MUSIC STAR

Born in south Texas, Johnny Rodriguez drew on mariachi music, honky tonk and the Great American Songbook. Imprisoned for a minor offence aged 18, he was heard singing in his cell by a Texas Ranger, who recommended Rodriguez to the man who became his manager. He moved to Nashville, landed a recording contract with Mercury Records and his first single 'Pass Me By (If You're Only Passing Through' (1972) reached No.9 in the *Billboard* country charts.

In 1973, Rodriguez landed his first chart-topping single with 'You Always Come Back (To Hurting Me)' and his debut album reached No.1. He embraced a smoother sound in 1975 and his next three singles were all No.1 hits.

In a quote from the PBS documentary *Country Music: A Film By Ken Burns*, Rodriguez outlined his attraction to country music. "I could relate more to what they were singing about," he said. "In Mexican music, you have stories. Mexican music and country music said almost the same thing, just in different languages."

COUNTRY MUSIC ICONS **69**

1932–2022

Essential Tracks

» YOU AIN'T WOMAN ENOUGH TO TAKE MY MAN

» COAL MINER'S DAUGHTER

» DON'T COME HOME A-DRINKIN' (WITH LOVIN' ON YOUR MIND)

LYNN WAS GOOD FRIENDS WITH PATSY CLINE, WHO DIED IN A PLANE CRASH IN 1963. "I STILL MISS HER TO THIS DAY," SAID LYNN IN 2009.

Loretta Lynn

LORETTA LYNN

POVERTY AND HEARTBREAK PERVADED THE SONGS OF LORETTA LYNN, WHO BECAME A DEFIANT VOICE FOR ORDINARY WOMEN ACROSS A STELLAR, SIX-DECADE CAREER

No country singer-songwriter has epitomised the authentic blue-collar voice of the American South quite as overwhelmingly as Loretta Lynn. Born into poverty in rural Kentucky, married at the age of 15 and a mother of four by the time she was 22, Lynn would go on to write songs about heartbreak and hardship that are some of the most celebrated in the genre of country music.

Over the course of a career spanning six decades, Lynn topped the US country charts 16 times, recorded 60 studio albums and was nominated for 18 Grammys, winning three.

She formed a band in 1953 called Loretta and the Trailblazers, began writing songs and released her debut single 'I'm a Honky Tonk Girl' in 1960. The song reached the country music Top 20 and she was signed by Decca.

Relationship break-ups would be a prevailing theme in her songs but the characters were defiant, strong women. Her self-penned single 'Success' (1962) became her first Top 10 country hit and a raft of No.1 singles on the US country chart followed. These included 'Don't Come Home a Drinkin' (With Lovin' on Your Mind)', which cemented her reputation as the defiant voice of the ordinary woman. In 1970, she released the autobiographical single 'Coal Miner's Daughter', which shot to No.1 on the *Billboard* US Country chart and became her signature song. Another No.1, 'Rated X', addressed the stigma of divorce, while 'The Pill' (1975), a celebration of birth control, crossed over into the mainstream pop charts.

From 1964 to 1976 Lynn released four albums a year and collaborated with other country stars, including ten duet albums with Conway Twitty and the 1993 album *Honky Tonk Angels* with Dolly Parton and Tammy Wynette.

In 2004, she had a high-profile resurgence with *Van Lear Rose*, an album produced by Jack White of The White Stripes. It became her bestselling record at that point, but was eclipsed in 2016 by *Full Circle*, which featured duets with Willie Nelson and Elvis Costello.

In 1976, Lynn wrote a successful biography entitled *Coal Miner's Daughter*, which was adapted for the big screen in 1980 and starred Sissy Spacek. Her 46th and final album, *Still Woman Enough* (2021), was released a year before her death, and featured 'Coal Miner's Daughter Recitation', a 50th anniversary celebration of her signature song.

LEFT LYNN'S CUSTOM EPIPHONE GUITAR FEATURED HER NAME ALONG THE FRETBOARD.

RIGHT PERFORMING AT THE BONNAROO MUSIC AND ARTS FESTIVAL IN 2011.

THE CHICKS

FORMED 1989

Essential Tracks
- COWBOY TAKE ME AWAY
- NOT READY TO MAKE NICE
- WIDE OPEN SPACES

THE CHICKS

THE CHICKS HAVE BECOME ONE OF COUNTRY MUSIC'S MOST SUCCESSFUL BANDS AND REDEFINED THE POLITICAL LANDSCAPE OF THE GENRE

Renamed from The Dixie Chicks in 2020, The Chicks originally formed in 1989 with sisters Emily and Martie and friends Laura Lynch and Robin Lyn Macey.

After Macey and Lynch left the band over the years, Natalie Maines joined and they released *Wide Open Spaces*. They enjoyed a bestselling and highly decorated career, with their bluegrass, pop and blues-infused country sound, tight harmonies and lively stage presence appealing to the masses.

Their success was briefly interrupted after they became a source of controversy in 2003. The band were vocal about their opposition to the Iraq War, prompting a boycott of their music and leading to a three year hiatus from the spotlight. When they returned, they did so with the multi-award winning album *Taking the Long Way*.

They are one of the most successful country bands of all time and set a new tone for country music's traditionally conservative, male image.

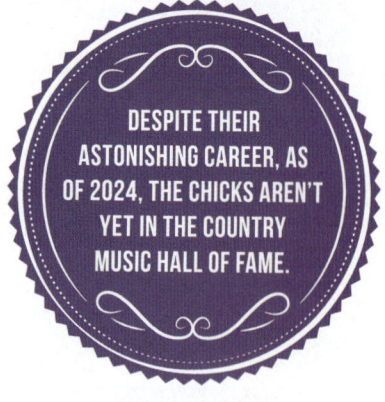

DESPITE THEIR ASTONISHING CAREER, AS OF 2024, THE CHICKS AREN'T YET IN THE COUNTRY MUSIC HALL OF FAME.

GLEN CAMPBELL

1936–2017

Essential Tracks
- WICHITA LINEMAN
- BY THE TIME I GET TO PHOENIX
- GENTLE ON MY MIND

ONE OF THE MOST SUCCESSFUL COUNTRY SINGERS OF HIS GENERATION WHO SPANNED THE COUNTRY AND POP MARKETS

Arkansas-born Glen Campbell started out as a session guitarist with legendary LA session collective the Wrecking Crew. He signed a solo deal with Capitol, had a modest hit with John Hartford's classic song 'Gentle on My Mind' and scored a Top 20 country hit with the album *Burning Bridges* in 1967.

But it was Campbell's collaboration with songwriter Jimmy Webb that really made an impact. Campbell's rendition of Webb's 'By the Time I Get to Phoenix' reached No.2 in the US country charts in 1967.

The follow-up 'Wichita Lineman' topped the country chart in May 1968 and hit No.3 in the mainstream *Billboard* 100 chart. This song, with its sweeping melancholy, became a timeless classic. Another Webb composition, 'Galveston', yielded a No.1 hit in 1969.

By 1970, Campbell was a huge star, with his own TV show and was moving into acting. By the mid-70s his style was middle-of-the-road and he scored a massive crossover hit with 'Rhinestone Cowboy' in 1974.

Campbell was one of the biggest stars of his era, spanning country and pop. He often acknowledged his debt to the songwriters such as Webb whose compositions produced such enduring hits.

CAMPBELL TOURED WITH THE BEACH BOYS IN 1965, REPLACING BRIAN WILSON WHO HAD RETIRED FROM PERFORMING.

COUNTRY MUSIC ICONS 73

1931–2013

> JONES WAS AWARDED THE PRESTIGIOUS KENNEDY CENTER HONORS FOR LIFETIME ACHIEVEMENT IN 2008.

GEORGE JONES

ONE OF THE MOST INFLUENTIAL SINGERS IN THE HISTORY OF COUNTRY MUSIC, WHOSE LIFE ECHOED THE STORIES WITHIN HIS SONGS

From 1955 to 2005, George Jones established himself as a towering figure within country music, the undisputed king of raw honky tonk with a direct lineage to Hank Williams, Ray Acuff and Ernest Tubbs. Jones' rich, emotionally wrought baritone made him one of the most influential singers in that genre. "In country music, George Jones set the standard long ago," Johnny Cash once said. "No one has compared to him yet."

Born into poverty in East Texas, with an abusive alcoholic father, Jones got his first guitar aged 11 and was busking by the age of 13. After serving in the US Marines, he scored his first country hit in 1955 with 'Why Baby Why' and enjoyed a long string of hits including 'White Lightning' (1959), 'Tender Years' (1961), 'She Thinks I Still Care' (1962), 'Walk Through This World with Me' (1967) and 'The Grand Tour' (1974), all of which reached No.1 in the US country charts.

He married Tammy Wynette in 1969, and the dramatic twists and turns of their relationship were reflected like a soap opera within their songs. They notched up eight duet hits between 1972 and 1975, while their gut-wrenching 1976 hit 'Golden Ring' catalogued their love affair, marriage and subsequent divorce.

Alcohol and cocaine abuse pervaded Jones' life in the 1970s, resulting in him missing some performances and earning the title 'No Show Jones'. But out of all the pain came 'He Stopped Loving Her Today', a poignant, mournful million-selling ballad with Jones' anguish-drenched vocals that hit No.1 in 1980 and earned Jones a Grammy for Best Male Country Vocal Performance.

The late 80s and 90s found Jones clean and sober and when he hit the bottle again in 1999 and had a near-fatal car crash, he turned to sacred music for the 2003 double album *The Gospel Collection: George Jones Sings the Greatest Stories Ever Told*.

Jones' profound talent was acknowledged beyond the world of country and his admirers included Frank Sinatra, James Taylor and The Who's Pete Townshend. Waylon Jennings spoke for many when he said: "If we could all sound like we wanted to, we would all sound like George Jones."

ABOVE JONES AT THE COUNTRY MUSIC HALL OF FAME AND MUSEUM IN 2011.

ABOVE RIGHT PERFORMING AT THE 1988 COUNTRY MUSIC ASSOCIATION AWARDS.

Essential Tracks
- HE STOPPED LOVING HER TODAY
- THE RACE IS ON
- THE GRAND TOUR

KEITH URBAN

1967–PRESENT

KEITH URBAN

A UNIQUE ARTIST WHOSE POP AND ROCK INFLUENCES HAVE HELPED ENSURE MASSIVE CROSSOVER SUCCESS

New Zealand-born Australian-American singer, songwriter and guitarist Keith Urban emerged in 1999 with a strong pop-rock influenced sound that put him on the periphery of the mainstream country music market.

Urban's 1999 self-titled debut album produced four hit singles and his 2002 follow-up, *Golden Road*, went triple platinum. He was making a name for himself in the music industry, but tabloid interest in this country superstar went stratospheric when he married actress Nicole Kidman in June 2006.

In 2017, he released the single 'Female', inspired by the #MeToo movement, which appeared on his electronica-influenced 2018 album *Graffiti U*. Duets with Julia Michaels and P!nk also yielded Top 10 hits, while his 11th studio album *The Speed Of Now* reached No.1 in the US Country chart.

Urban has been festooned with awards but one of country music's highest honours was bestowed in 2012 when he was inducted into the Grand Ole Opry. He was clearly moved by this honour. "It truly has been the most magical night of my life," he said.

IN 1983, URBAN WAS A CONTESTANT ON THE AUSTRALIAN TV TALENT SHOW *NEW FACES*.

Essential Tracks

- YOU'LL THINK OF ME
- SOMEBODY LIKE YOU
- BUT FOR THE GRACE OF GOD

1947–PRESENT

HUGELY INFLUENTIAL WITHIN AMERICANA AND COUNTRY-ROCK, HARRIS REMAINS A STRONG CREATIVE FORCE IN CONTEMPORARY MUSIC

Essential Tracks

- RED DIRT GIRL
- BOULDER TO BIRMINGHAM
- BENEATH STILL WATERS

HARRIS WAS A STRAIGHT-A STUDENT AND PLAYED SAXOPHONE IN THE HIGH SCHOOL MARCHING BAND.

EMMYLOU HARRIS

Emmylou Harris was singing folk songs in a Washington DC club when singer-songwriter Gram Parsons sought her out for her sublime, crystalline vocals, which she contributed to his solo albums, *G.P.* (1972) and *Grievous Angel* (1974).

Parsons introduced her to country music and following his death in 1973, Harris embarked on a solo career. Her second album, *Elite Hotel* (1973), topped the US Country charts and featured covers of Buck Owens' 'Together Again' and Patsy Cline's 'Sweet Dreams'. *Luxury Liner* (1977) also peaked at No.1 in the US country chart.

Across her career, Harris has been an adventurous creative spirit, as demonstrated on the full-on acoustic bluegrass of the 1980 album *Roses in the Snow*. In 1987 she teamed up with Dolly Parton and Linda Ronstadt for *Trio*, which was Harris's most successful album to date.

Another high point was 1995's *Wrecking Ball*, a stunningly beautiful work on which she performed songs by Neil Young and Gillian Welch, among others. The album *Red Dirt Girl* (2000) showcased her songwriting skills and won her the Grammy for Best Contemporary Folk Album in 2001.

Harris continues to be a towering, iconic figure within country music. In 2008, she was justifiably inducted into the Country Music Hall of Fame, and in 2018, she was presented with a Grammy Lifetime Achievement Award.

1923–1953

HANK WILLIAMS

IN JUST 30 SHORT YEARS, HANK WILLIAMS LIVED A COLOURFUL AND COMPLICATED LIFE

Born in Mount Olive, Alabama, on 17 September 1923 to Elonzo and Jessie "Lillie" Williams, Hiram "Hank" Williams' childhood took place against the backdrop of a complicated family life. He was born with spina bifida occulta, a condition that caused him lifelong pain. His father was also absent during most of his childhood due to his own health issues, so his mother assumed the role of head of the household.

Williams received his first musical instrument, a harmonica, when he was just six years old, and the family moved to Georgiana, Alabama, where he began to play guitar at the age of eight. The family later moved again to Montgomery where a teenage Hank sang his first original song, 'WPA Blues' at a talent show and eventually ended up performing on air at WSFA radio.

Williams formed his band, the Drifting Cowboys, managed by his mother, and dropped out of school to perform with the band full-time. He struggled with alcoholism, which caused many band members to quit. Things came to a head in 1942 when he was fired from WSFA and so he began working as a shipfitter's helper that year. He met a fellow shipyard worker, Audrey Sheppard, in 1943, and they were married the following year.

In 1946, Williams travelled to Nashville where he met music publisher Fred Rose, with whom he signed his first record deal. He recorded successful songs including 'Never Again (Will I Knock on Your Door)'. He later signed with MGM Records and topped the *Billboard* charts with his version of 'Lovesick Blues', kicking off a string of hits.

Despite this success, Williams' faced personal struggles. In May 1951, he was hospitalised in an attempt to treat him for back problems and alcoholism. He later had an affair with dancer Bobbie Jett, which arguably led to his divorce from Audrey in 1952.

In June that year, Williams recorded some of his most famous songs, including 'Jambalaya (On the Bayou)'. He married his second wife, fellow singer-songwriter Billie Jean Jones, in October 1952. At the time, he had continued to suffer from alcohol and substance abuse, and Williams sadly died from heart failure on his way to a concert on New Year's Day, 1953.

LEFT WILLIAMS PICTURED WITH HIS BAND, THE DRIFTING COWBOYS, IN 1951.

Essential Tracks

- HEY, GOOD LOOKIN'
- JAMBALAYA (ON THE BAYOU)
- YOUR CHEATIN' HEART

HANK WILLIAMS

WILLIAMS IS WIDELY REGARDED AS THE FIRST PERSON TO ACHIEVE COUNTRY MUSIC SUPERSTARDOM.

"
WILLIAMS TOPPED THE *BILLBOARD* CHARTS WITH HIS VERSION OF 'LOVESICK BLUES'

COUNTRY MUSIC ICONS 79

Life & Career

Part-time philosopher
Alongside his more popular songs, Williams recorded music that explored the themes of philosophy and morality. Fred Rose wanted to ensure Williams' more commercially viable songs would be played on jukeboxes and so the recordings were published under a pseudonym, Luke the Drifter. Of course, he still performed some of these songs at his shows, lamenting questions of societal injustice and death.

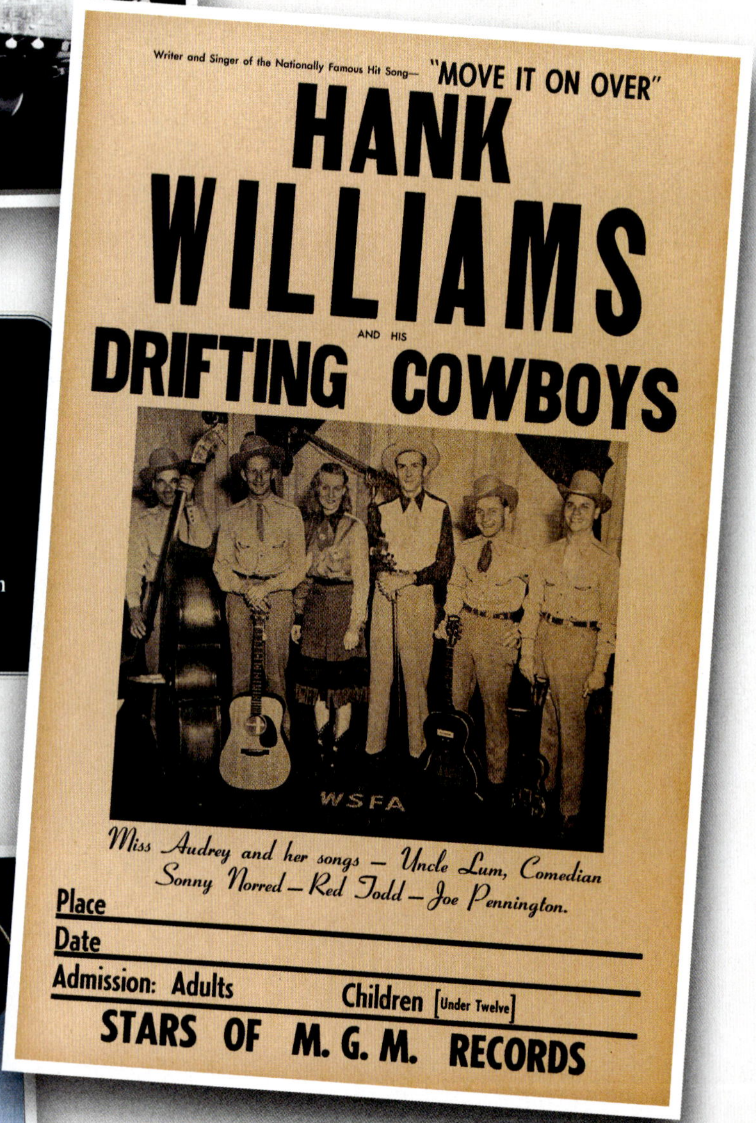

Budding songwriter
Williams published his first songbook in 1945, called *Original Songs of Hank Williams*. It allowed him to really make a name for himself as a songwriter, with nine original songs including 'I Am Praying for the Day that Peace Will Come', 'Honkey-Tonkey' and 'Won't You Please Come Back'. Another song that he had not written himself was included, called 'A Tramp on the Street'.

Self-destructive struggles
Williams struggled with alcohol throughout his adult life, largely believed to have been an attempt at self-medication for severe back pain he suffered due to his spina bifida. After an unsuccessful back surgery, he also became addicted to painkillers. These addiction issues led to members of his band quitting, missed or poor performances, and his dismissal from WSFA radio and the Grand Ole Opry. Earlier in his career, he met fellow country singer Roy Acuff, who urged him to consider the repercussions of his alcoholism, saying "You've got a million-dollar voice, son, but a ten-cent brain".

HANK WILLIAMS

ABOVE A 1949 WILLIAMS FAMILY PORTRAIT, WITH HIS FIRST WIFE, AUDREY, HER DAUGHTER, LYCRECIA, AND THEIR BABY SON, HANK JR.

WILLIAMS FAILED HIS FIRST GRAND OLE OPRY AUDITION IN 1946, BUT MADE HIS SUCCESSFUL DEBUT THREE YEARS LATER.

A pivotal mentor

Williams' early introduction to music was heavily influenced by an African-American street performer called Rufus "Tee-Tot" Payne, based in Georgiana, Alabama. He taught Williams how to play guitar as he immersed him in the blues genre. Payne taught Hank in return for cash or meals, but he lost touch with the Williams family when they moved to Montgomery. Their relationship was indirectly referenced in the 2011 dramatisation, *The Last Ride* (pictured).

COUNTRY MUSIC ICONS **81**

KENNY RODGERS

1938–2020

Essential Tracks
» MOUNTAIN MUSIC
» FEELS SO RIGHT
» THERE'S NO WAY

IN 1985, ROGERS WAS ONE OF THE FEATURED STARS ON USA FOR AFRICA'S 'WE ARE THE WORLD'.

Kenny Rogers

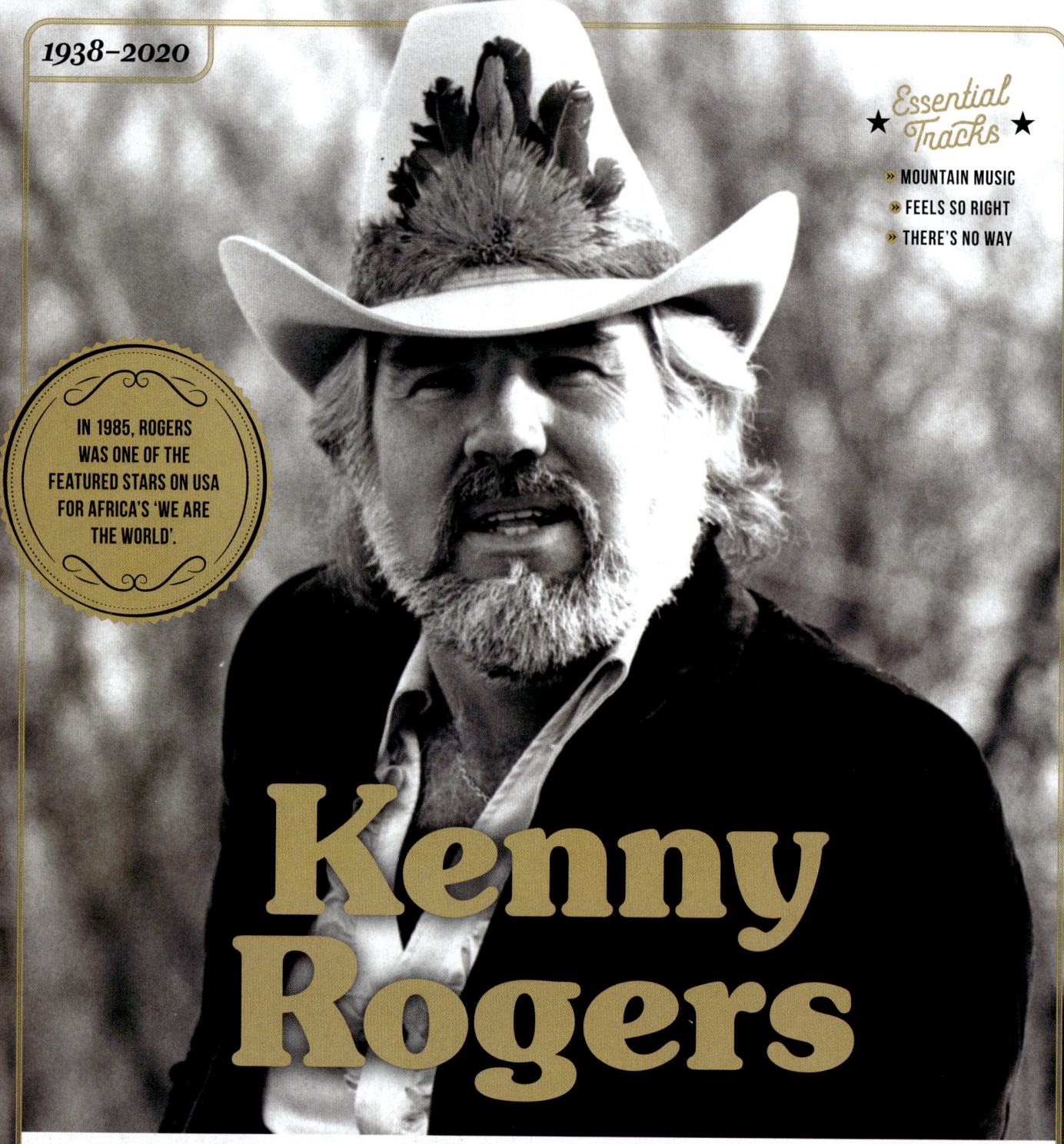

A PROLIFIC HITMAKER AND A COUNTRY MUSIC GREAT, KENNY ROGERS WAS A GRAVEL-VOICED COLOSSUS OF THE COUNTRY SCENE

From the late 1960s to the 80s, Kenny Rogers was one of the great country singers, with a stream of narrative-based singles such as 'Lucille' (1977), 'The Gambler' (1978) and 'Coward of the County' (1979). He had an easy, gravel-voiced style and a talent for finding songs that suited it, such as Lionel Richie's 'Lady' (1978) and The Bee Gees' 'Islands in the Stream', which he recorded as a duet with Dolly Parton in 1983.

Rogers emerged with *The First Edition*, whose single 'Ruby, Don't Take Your Love to Town' (1969) became a Top 10 hit in both the US and UK. By the 80s, Rogers spanned pop and country. His duet with Sheena Easton, 'We've Got Tonight' (1983), topped the *Billboard* Hot Country chart and reached No.6 on the *Billboard* Hot 100 chart.

By the 80s Rogers was successfully diversifying into acting roles. He and Parton performed together for decades, and had a special bond. "I love him to death," Parton told broadcaster Dan Rather in 2017. "He's like a brother to me, or like a twin soul."

LINDA MARTELL

1941–PRESENT

AFTER SHE RETIRED FROM MUSIC, MARTELL BECAME A PUBLIC SCHOOL BUS DRIVER.

Essential Tracks
- BAD CASE OF THE BLUES
- COLOR HIM FATHER
- BEFORE THE NEXT TEARDROP FALLS

A PIONEER AND TRAILBLAZER, MARTELL BECAME THE FIRST COMMERCIALLY SUCCESSFUL BLACK FEMALE COUNTRY ARTIST

Linda Martell grew up in Leesville, South Carolina, singing gospel music at church and performing with her band, The Anglos, but fell in love with country music after listening to Hank Williams on the radio. She met her manager, William "Duke" Rayner, after he heard her sing during a performance on an air base, and she began to cultivate her style with flourishes of balladry, gospel and R&B.

Martell released just one album, *Color Me Country* (1970), and broke down barriers for other Black artists by appearing on the popular country show *Hee Haw*. Unfortunately, she suffered awful racist abuse from audiences during her live performances, and Martell had to cut ties with her record label, Plantation, when they chose to prioritise the white country-pop singer, Jeannie C Riley. In her words, Martell was then "blacklisted", and eventually had to retire from music.

There has been a resurgence in interest in Martell over the last few years, particularly since she featured on two tracks from Beyoncé's country album, *Cowboy Carter* (2024).

1942–1998

Tammy Wynette

WYNETTE WAS INDUCTED INTO THE COUNTRY MUSIC HALL OF FAME IN 1998.

TAMMY WYNETTE

Essential Tracks

- D-I-V-O-R-C-E
- STAND BY YOUR MAN
- 'TIL I CAN MAKE IT ON MY OWN

QUEEN OF COUNTRY TAMMY WYNETTE BROUGHT FEMALE PERSPECTIVES TO THE FORE OF THE GENRE WITH A PROLIFIC RUN OF CLASSIC HITS

Widely regarded as one of the most successful and influential female vocalists in the history of country music, Tammy Wynette was a uniquely creative singer-songwriter who helped push women's perspectives to the fore in the then overwhelmingly male-dominated country music scene.

Born Virginia Wynette Pugh in Mississippi, she picked cotton on her parents' farm but dreamed of becoming a country singer. She turned professional in 1965, at the age of 23. By then, she was divorced from her first husband and raising three children. She approached record labels in Nashville and in 1966, Epic Records producer Billy Sherrill signed her. Wynette's first single was 'Apartment Number Nine', a modest hit, while the follow-up 'Your Good Girl's Gonna Be Bad' (1967) made the Top 10.

Wynette landed her first No.1 with 'I Don't Wanna Play House' but the song that really resonated with the public was 'D-I-V-O-R-C-E' (1968), which shot to No.1 on the *Billboard* Hot Country Singles chart. "I hated myself for not writing that song," recalled Wynette. "It fit my life completely."

But Wynette would co-write her best-known song 'Stand by Your Man', reportedly written by Wynette and Billy Sherrill in 15 minutes. The song reached No.1 in the *Billboard* Hot Country Singles chart and No.1 in the UK Singles chart. The album of the same name received widespread critical acclaim.

> **WYNETTE'S LIFE WAS FILLED WITH HEARTBREAK AND DRAMA**

In 1969, Wynette married fellow country singer George Jones, and they recorded a string of duets that catalogued their tempestuous relationship.

Ten more No.1 hits followed, such as 'Good Lovin' (Makes It Right) (1971) 'Kids Say the Darndest Things' (1973) and the wonderfully poignant "Til I Can Make It on My Own' (1976).

By the end of the 1980s, Wynette had racked up 20 chart-topping singles and sold 30 million albums. An unexpected collaboration with British duo The KLF in 1991 produced an international dance hit 'Justified & Ancient'.

Her life was filled with heartbreak and drama, but Wynette was a torchbearer for women in country music. Musically, she left a powerful legacy. As Randy Travis put it: "Lots of entertainers have recorded a few good songs but Tammy's many hits will be around long after the others are forgotten".

ABOVE WYNETTE PICTURED WITH FELLOW COUNTRY MUSIC STAR CHARLEY PRIDE.

RIGHT ON STAGE DURING THE COUNTRY MUSIC FESTIVAL IN LONDON, 1981.

TIM MCGRAW

1967–PRESENT

TIM MCGRAW

A HONKY-TONK SINGER SPANNING COUNTRY AND STADIUM ROCK WHO HAS DOMINATED THE COUNTRY AND MAINSTREAM CHARTS

★ *Essential Tracks* ★
» LIVE LIKE YOU WERE DYING
» I LIKE IT, I LOVE IT
» SOMETHING LIKE THAT

It has been 30 years since Tim McGraw had his first No.1 hit with 'Don't Take the Girl' from his second album *Not a Moment Too Soon* and joined a new generation of stadium-rocking country superstars.

As of June 2024, McGraw has sold more than 90 million records, racking up 46 No.1 singles and 19 chart-topping albums worldwide. Then there are the accolades: he has received three Grammys, 21 Academy of Country Music Awards and 14 Country Music Association Awards.

Stylistically, McGraw specialises in heartfelt ballads and like many of his platinum-selling contemporaries, effortlessly spans both the country and pop charts.

In 1996, he married Faith Hill and this country music power duo's Soul2Soul tours have set new records on the live circuit. McGraw is also an acclaimed actor, having appeared in major films and TV series, such as *Dirty Girl* (2010), *Tomorrowland* (2015) and *1883* (2021-22).

While his mainstream chart placings may have diminished slightly in the last few years, his 16th album, *Standing Room Only* (2023), still reached No.4 on the US Hot Country Songs chart.

> MCGRAW WAS THE NAMESAKE OF TAYLOR SWIFT'S 2006 DEBUT SINGLE. SHE ENDED UP SUPPORTING HIM ON TOUR THE FOLLOWING YEAR.

ALISON KRAUSS

1971–PRESENT

KRAUSS IS ONE OF THE MOST PROLIFIC GRAMMY WINNERS, SECOND ONLY TO BEYONCÉ AMONG FEMALE ARTISTS.

Essential Tracks
- WHEN YOU SAY NOTHING AT ALL
- DOWN TO THE RIVER TO PRAY
- LET ME TOUCH YOU FOR A WHILE

ALISON KRAUSS

A GIFTED VOCALIST AND FIDDLER, KRAUSS IS ONE OF THE MOST INFLUENTIAL BLUEGRASS ARTISTS OF OUR TIME

When the Coen Brothers' film *Oh Brother Where Art Thou?* was released in 2000, it catapulted bluegrass music into the mainstream. This made superstars of artists such as Alison Krauss, whose graceful, captivating music featured prominently on the soundtrack.

In truth, Illinois-born Krauss was already a star thanks to her second album, the acclaimed 1995 compilation *Now That I've Found You*, which showcased her emotive vocals and fiddle-playing prowess. The album reached No.2 on the country charts and crossed over into the pop Top 10.

In 2001 Krauss and the band Union Station released the album *New Favourite*, which went gold. A live record followed, and in 2007 her collaboration with former Led Zeppelin rocker Robert Plant yielded the album *Raising Sand*, a critically acclaimed platinum-selling collaboration.

Vocal problems and relentless touring delayed the release of *Windy City* (2017), a collection of covers of classic tunes. In 2021, Krauss and Plant reunited for the album *Raise the Roof*, released to universal acclaim, and embarked on a tour as a duo the following year.

Krauss' unassuming persona belies her considerable achievements – 27 Grammy Award wins of 44 nominations so far, and over 12 million albums sold as of May 2024.

COUNTRY MUSIC ICONS 87

1937–2002

WAYLON JENNINGS

A MUSICAL REBEL AND A LEADING FIGURE IN THE COUNTRY SCENE, JENNINGS HELPED FORGE THE GRITTIER GENRE KNOWN AS OUTLAW COUNTRY MUSIC

Had events conspired differently, Waylon Jennings would have left this world on 3 February 1959, when the light aircraft carrying Buddy Holly, Ritchie Valens and JP Richardson, aka 'The Big Bopper', crashed in bad weather killing all on board. Jennings, Holly's friend and bass player, was due to be on the plane but gave up his seat for Richardson, who was ill.

Jennings felt profound survivor's guilt for years. In the decades that followed, he would make his mark as a solo artist, selling over 40 million records and revitalising country music with his bold new 'outlaw country' sound.

Texas-born Jennings learned to play guitar aged 12, and at 18 he landed a job as a radio DJ in Lubbock. There, he met Holly, who produced Jennings' first single, 'Jole Blon'. In the early 60s Jennings was recommended to Chet Atkins, who signed him to RCA in Nashville.

Jennings scored Top 10 hits with songs such as 'The Chokin' Kind' (1967) and 'Only Daddy That'll Walk the Line' (1968). But he resented what he saw as RCA's tight rein on him.

Jennings wanted to choose his own music and musicians, and eventually got his way with his 1973 albums *Lonesome, On'ry and Mean* and *Honky Tonk Heroes*.

His 1975 chart-topping album *Dreaming My Dreams* yielded the distinctive single 'Are You Sure Hank Did It This Way?', a No.1 hit that takes a critical swipe at the glitz and sheen of the 70s country music scene. But it was the colossal sales of the 1976 album *Wanted! The Outlaws* – featuring Jennings, Willie Nelson, Jessi Colter, and Tompall Glaser – that really shook things up in Nashville. The album yielded the major crossover hit 'Good Hearted Woman' (1976).

In 1978, Jennings and Nelson, now billed as 'Waylon and Willie' released the single 'Mammas Don't Let Your Babies Grow Up to Be Cowboys', which won a Grammy for Best Country Vocal Performance by a Duo or Group.

In 1985, he joined Johnny Cash, Willie Nelson and Kris Kristofferson in 'country supergroup' The Highwaymen, whose first record reached No.1 in *Billboard*'s Top Country Albums. By then, Jennings was spending $1,500 a day on cocaine; he kicked the habit and also stopped smoking, but the years of excess contributed to serious health problems towards the end of his life. He scaled things down for some of his finest work, the albums *Waymore's Blues Part II* (1994) and *Right for the Time* (1996). One year before his death, he was made a member of the Country Music Hall of Fame but declined to attend the ceremony.

Like many great artists, Jennings stayed true to his creative vision and refused to compromise. In the process, he revitalised country music and left a rich, enduring legacy.

JENNINGS WROTE THE THEME SONG TO THE TELEVISION SERIES *THE DUKES OF HAZZARD*.

WAYLON JENNINGS

Essential Tracks
» ARE YOU SURE HANK DONE IT THIS WAY?
» HONKY TONK HEROES
» MAMMAS DON'T LET YOUR BABIES GROW UP TO BE COWBOYS

BOTTOM LEFT
JENNINGS PIONEERED THE OUTLAW AND PROGRESSIVE COUNTRY SUBGENRES.

BOTTOM RIGHT
JENNINGS AND BUDDY HOLLY PICTURED IN 1959, NOT LONG BEFORE THE LATTER DIED IN A PLANE CRASH.

" JENNINGS RESENTED WHAT HE SAW AS RCA'S TIGHT REIN ON HIM. HE WANTED TO CHOOSE HIS OWN MUSIC AND MUSICIANS

COUNTRY MUSIC ICONS 89

FORMED 1998

Essential Tracks
- GIRL CRUSH
- BOONDOCKS
- BETTER MAN

little big town

THIS QUARTET HAVE BEEN CONTINUALLY PROVIDING A FRESH SOUND TO COUNTRY MUSIC FOR DECADES

LITTLE BIG TOWN WERE THE FIRST ACT TO EVER HAVE A RESIDENCY AT LEGENDARY RYMAN AUDITORIUM IN NASHVILLE.

Little Big Town has consisted of the same four members since the band's inception: Karen Fairchild, Kimberly Schlapman, Phillip Sweet, and Jimi Westbrook. They're a tight-knit group: Fairchild and Westbrook married in 2013, and the band have joked that their longevity has been due to their enduring friendships.

Their early career was punctuated with support shows for the likes of Carrie Underwood and Sugarland and they faced setbacks with their changing record companies throughout the 2000s. In 2010 their luck changed with a series of charting hits and albums, and soon gave way to their most commercially successful and critically acclaimed album to date, 2014's *Pain Killer*.

Little Big Town famously does not have a lead: the four members rotate through leading vocals across their catalogue. The band's tracks are easily identifiable by their silky four-way harmonies. Their songwriting is carefully crafted to create their infectious sing-a-long lyrics and the storytelling country music is renowned for.

JASON ALDEAN

1977–PRESENT

Essential Tracks

- DON'T YOU WANNA STAY (WITH KELLY CLARKSON)
- 'IF I DIDN'T LOVE YOU' (WITH CARRIE UNDERWOOD)
- TROUBLE WITH A HEARTBREAK

JASON ALDEAN

CHART-TOPPING BRO-COUNTRY VIBES FROM ONE OF THE MOST FORTHRIGHT VOICES IN MODERN COUNTRY

Jason Aldine Williams was born in Macon, Georgia and was taught to play country songs on guitar by his dad. He was performing on stage by the age of 14 and signed a record deal after a move to Nashville in 1998. To differentiate himself from the famous basketball player also called Jason Williams, he created a stage name using the altered spelling of Aldean.

It took a while for success to come Aldean's way, but in 2005 he had his first No.1 with 'Why' and the rest was essentially history, with a strong sequence of award-winning albums and chart-topping singles following over the years.

Career high points have included 2008's 'She's Country' hit, a performance with none other than Bryan Adams on an episode of *CMT Crossroads* the following year and a collaboration with Kelly Clarkson in 2010.

Aldean drew controversy in 2023 after his No.1 hit, 'Try That in a Small Town', and its accompanying video led to accusations of racism, which he strenuously denied.

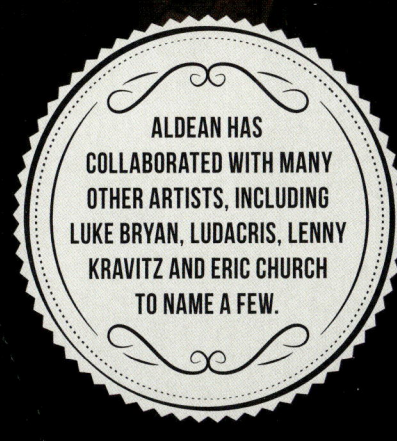

> ALDEAN HAS COLLABORATED WITH MANY OTHER ARTISTS, INCLUDING LUKE BRYAN, LUDACRIS, LENNY KRAVITZ AND ERIC CHURCH TO NAME A FEW.

COUNTRY MUSIC ICONS 91

1965–PRESENT

SHANIA

WARM, WITTY AND WILFUL: SHANIA TWAIN CHANGED THE FACE OF COUNTRY MUSIC AND ROSE TO UNPRECEDENTED LEVELS OF SUCCESS

Born Eilleen Edwards in Ontario, Canada, Shania Twain saw singing as a means of escape from a turbulent childhood. She delayed her career to raise her siblings, eventually signing to Mercury Nashville Records and releasing her debut album, *Shania Twain*, in 1993.

Her debut's mild success garnered some international attention, notably from producer Robert Lange. The pair met and quickly became collaborators and married. Twain and Lange co-wrote most of her second album, *The Woman in Me*, with a fine-tuned country-pop sound, and catapulted Twain to success. Sentimental, tinged with rock and pop and carried by her powerful vocals, the album enjoyed both critical and commercial success.

Riding high on the accolades and commercial hits, Twain's international breakthrough came with 1997's *Come On Over*. The album went stratospheric, with mega-hits 'That Don't Impress Me Much' and 'You're Still the One' skyrocketing through the charts and into rarefied pop legend territory. The album became – and remains – the biggest-selling studio record of all time for a female artist, and its impact on pop culture is still felt today.

Riding high on this success, Twain released *Up!* in 2002, which was certified 11 times platinum, followed by a *Greatest Hits* collection two years later. However, this string of hits was interrupted by an extended absence induced by her struggle with Lyme disease and dysphonia, which threatened her

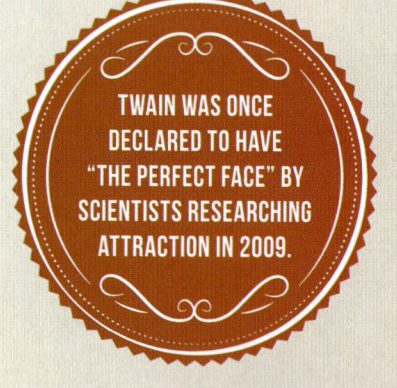

> **TWAIN WAS ONCE DECLARED TO HAVE "THE PERFECT FACE" BY SCIENTISTS RESEARCHING ATTRACTION IN 2009.**

LEFT TWAIN PICTURED AT THE GRAMMYS IN 1999 WITH HER TWO TROPHIES FOR 'YOU'RE STILL THE ONE'.

Essential Tracks
- MAN! I FEEL LIKE A WOMAN!
- YOU'RE STILL THE ONE
- WHOSE BED HAVE YOUR BOOTS BEEN UNDER?

TWAIN

ability to sing, and was compounded by the breakdown of her marriage. She returned to the spotlight in 2012 with her Shania: Still the One two-year residency in Las Vegas, followed by a tour in 2015. In 2017, she released her fifth album, *Now*, followed by 2023's *Queen of Me*.

Twain's back catalogue is synonymous with a female empowerment message. Alongside her yearning love songs, Twain became known for her playful lyrics and feminist undertones. This proto-feminism concerned the conservative country management boardrooms at the time, but actually drove the genre forwards. She's credited with paving the way for a host of female country artists to come, and remains one of the most commercially successful female country artists of all time.

> " **TWAIN DELAYED HER CAREER TO RAISE HER SIBLINGS**

LIFE & CAREER

›› World record holder

Shania Twain holds the Guinness World Record for the astonishing feat of having the biggest-selling female studio album of all time, with over 40 million copies of her breakout album *Come On Over* sold globally. This makes it the ninth bestselling album of all time. The album is second only to Morgan Wallen's *Dangerous* in best-ever country album chart performance, with almost an entire year sat atop the chart.

HER NAME 'SHANIA' WAS INSPIRED BY HER STEPFATHER'S INDIGENOUS ROOTS: MEANING 'ON MY WAY'.

SHANIA TWAIN

Iconic influencer

Artists ranging from Rihanna to Harry Styles and Post Malone have all credited Shania with influencing their music. Taylor Swift and Carrie Underwood have also acknowledged how Twain's impact on country music enabled them to pursue their own success in the industry. Twain seems keen on encouraging this part of her legacy: she has supported the careers and performed with many young artists, including country's Kelsea Ballerini and Orville Peck.

> **TWAIN HAS BEEN HONOURED WITH SOME OF COUNTRY MUSIC'S HIGHEST ACCOLADES**

Lifetime achievements

Twain's phenomenal commercial success is set against a backdrop of critical acclaim. In addition to breaking multiple records, Twain has been honoured with some of country music's highest accolades. This includes becoming the first non-US citizen to secure the coveted Entertainer of the Year at the CMA Awards. She was also the first woman to receive the CMT Artist of a Lifetime honour. She was inducted into the Nashville Songwriters Hall of Fame in 2022.

Overcoming tragedy

Twain was arguably at her peak when disaster struck: she lost her voice. This wasn't a simple case of a sore throat, she developed Lyme disease, devastating her vocal cords. She counts herself lucky, as the disease can have fatal consequences, but it certainly grounded her career from its almighty highs. Twain didn't produce new music for 15 years, eventually undertaking a laryngoplasty surgery to reconstruct her vocals. Overcoming the disease resuscitated her career for a new generation.

COUNTRY MUSIC ICONS

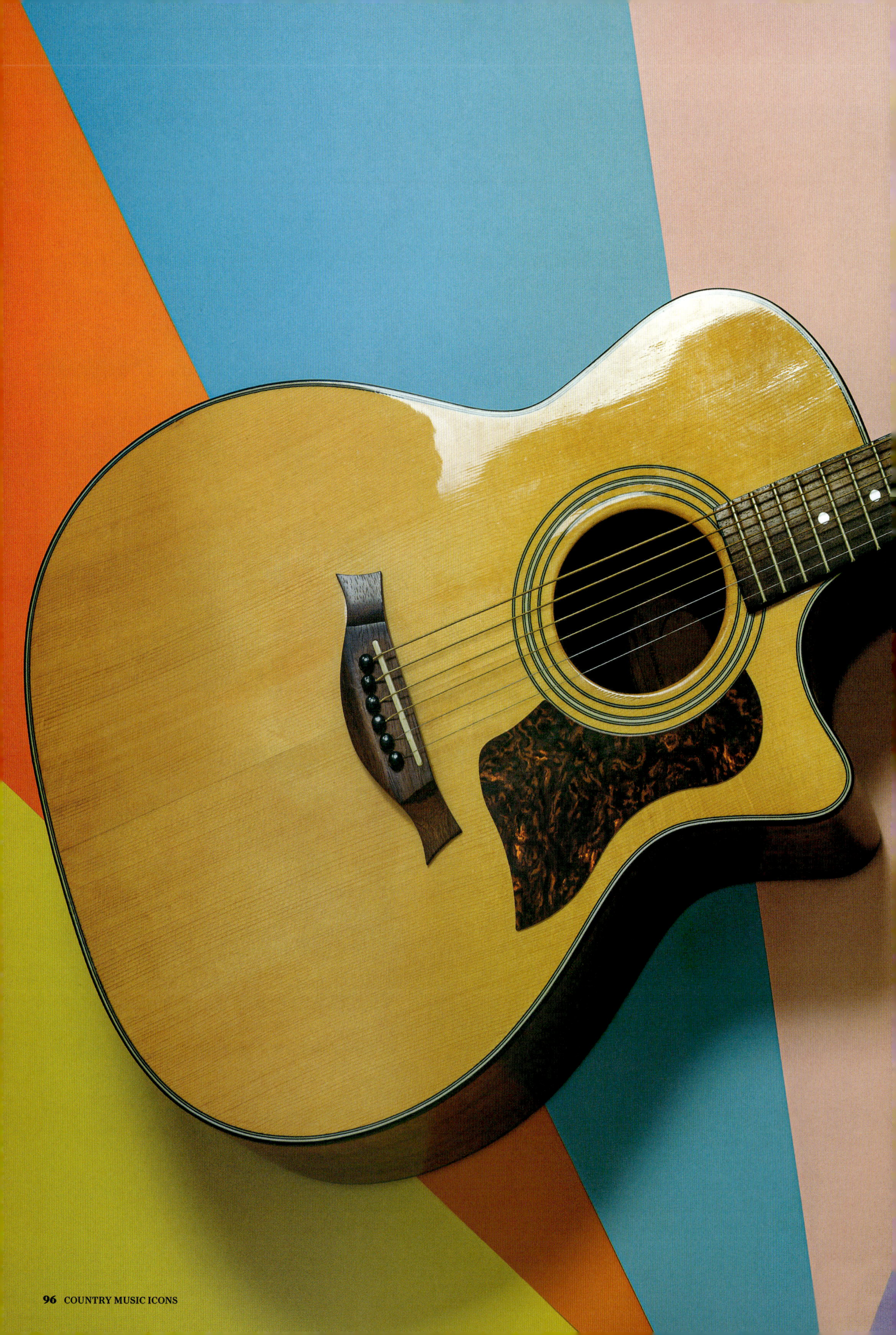

MODERN Country ★STARS★

DISCOVER THE ARTISTS WHO HAVE BROUGHT THE GENRE INTO THE 21ST CENTURY

98 Country's new horizons
HOW HAS AMERICA'S TRADITIONAL SOUND REBRANDED ITSELF FOR TODAY'S LISTENERS?

102 Carrie Underwood	**112** Kane Brown	**119** Chris Stapleton
104 Lainey Wilson	**113** Kelsea Ballerini	**120** Rascal Flatts
105 Miranda Lambert	**114** Mickey Guyton	**122** Allison Russell
106 Taylor Swift	**115** Lady A	**123** Maren Morris
108 Luke Combs	**116** Kacey Musgraves	**124** Zac Brown Band
109 Eric Church	**118** Morgan Wallen	**125** Luke Bryan
110 Darius Rucker		**126** Blake Shelton

Country's NEW HORIZONS

HOW HAS AMERICA'S TRADITIONAL SOUND REBRANDED ITSELF FOR TODAY'S LISTENERS?

Asked for his thoughts on the modern country artists of the day back in 2009, the 77-year-old country legend George Jones remarked with understandable bitterness: "They've stolen our identity… What they need to do is find their own title, because they're definitely not traditional country music."

In saying this, the late Jones was summarising a debate that had been raging since the 80s, when country music first began to incorporate new influences into its sound and spread to a wider demographic, both in terms of those who recorded it and those who consumed it. In the last two decades, this change in the face and feel of the genre has accelerated dramatically, with its commercial side as much – or more – pop than country, triggering the rise of a revitalised, 'authentic' flavour of the genre that sticks conservatively to the old sound. Of course, both sides are equally valid and both come from the same source, but that hasn't stopped battle lines being drawn.

You can point to several examples of the 'popification' – and 'rockification', while we're at it – of country music. In 2001, metal and rap artist Kid Rock scored a major country-rock hit in 'Picture' with the singer-songwriter Sheryl Crow that was somewhere between mainstream radio fodder and country; Darius Rucker of Hootie & the Blowfish switched from arena rock to country around the same time; while Carrie Underwood won the fourth season of *American Idol* in 2005 and

COUNTRY'S NEW HORIZONS

RIGHT CARRIE UNDERWOOD IS ONE OF MODERN COUNTRY'S BIGGEST STARS, AND HAS HAD HUGE MAINSTREAM SUCCESS.

FAR RIGHT BEYONCÉ'S *COWBOY CARTER* INTRODUCED NEW AUDIENCES — PARTICULARLY YOUNGER FANS — TO COUNTRY.

went stratospheric, becoming one of the genre's biggest stars.

However, even Underwood is a mere minnow, commercially speaking, compared to the ultimate country-goes-pop artist, Taylor Swift. A talented teenager who moved to Nashville to build a career, scored massively from day one and has never looked back, Swift is not only the most successful country-related star ever, she's in the top handful of artists of any genre of all time. Her billionaire status and vast cultural

ABOVE THE BRO-COUNTRY SUBGENRE BECAME POPULAR IN THE 2010S, LED BY FLORIDA GEORGIA LINE'S HIT 'CRUISE'.

MAIN LUKE BRYAN PERFORMING AT STAGECOACH IN 2023. THE EVENT IS ONE OF THE WORLD'S BIGGEST COUNTRY MUSIC FESTIVALS.

COUNTRY MUSIC ICONS 99

LIL NAS X'S 2019 HIT 'OLD TOWN ROAD,' A COUNTRY-TRAP MASHUP, TOPPED MAINSTREAM SINGLES CHARTS IN OVER TEN DIFFERENT COUNTRIES.

ABOVE IN 2019, LIL NAS X BECAME THE FIRST PERSON OF COLOUR AND FIRST OPENLY GAY ARTIST TO FEATURE IN *FORBES*' HIGHEST PAID COUNTRY ACTS LIST.

LEFT NASHVILLE'S PRIDE FESTIVAL IS THE BIGGEST LGBTQ+ EVENT IN THE STATE.

impact underline how profitable it can be to combine a banjo, a wailing violin and lyrics that tell a story set against catchy pop beats.

The equal and opposite reaction to country-pop has come with the rise of neotraditional country, music that is conservative in sound and often in its politics, too, although this is not universally the case. Less than keen on mashups such as country-trap (hip-hop beats with country themes like Blanco Brown's 2019 hit 'The Git Up') artists such as Jake Owen, Luke Bryan, Jason Aldean and Florida Georgia Line perform what is nicknamed 'bro-country'. Discussing topics such as partying, drinking, trucks and girls, the songs are reductive but popular, although they can be very blokey, as Maddie & Tae's No.1 hit response 'Girl in a Country Song' made very clear back in 2014.

Still, there has been progress on the left wing, with popular events such as Nashville Pride and the Celebrate Nashville Cultural Festival making it clear that all forms of country are for everyone to enjoy. Modern country songs often address subjects such as the LGBTQ+ community, religious agnosticism and safe sexual practices, and why the heck not? Country music must and will evolve, just as every form of music does, so let's enjoy the ride.

RIGHT TAYLOR SWIFT ROSE TO FAME AS A COUNTRY ARTIST, BEFORE BECOMING ONE OF THE WORLD'S BIGGEST POP STARS.

BELOW THE CMT NEXT WOMEN OF COUNTRY CLASS OF 2024 PORTRAIT. THE FRANCHISE HIGHLIGHTS FEMALE ARTISTS IN THE TRADITIONALLY MALE-DOMINATED GENRE.

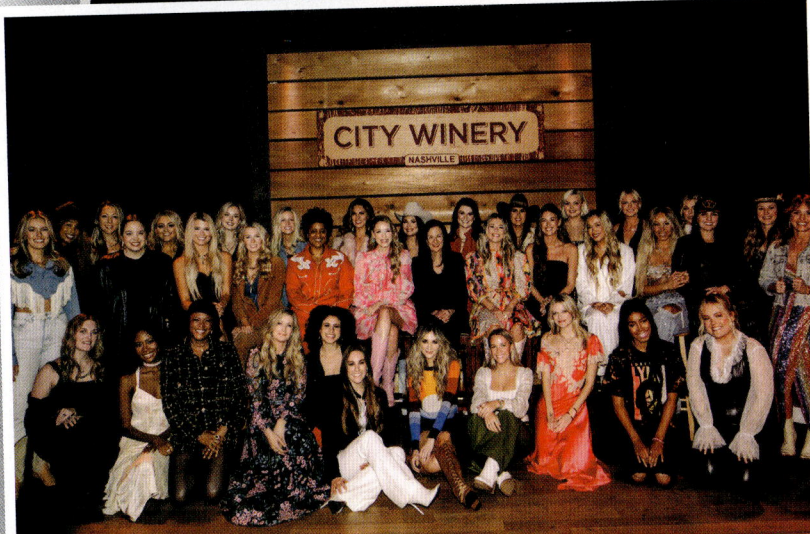

» How TV helped to spawn country-pop

Carrie Underwood may be *American Idol*'s best-known country-pop star, but she's not the only *Idol* export: the show has also given us Kristy Lee Cook, Kellie Pickler, Bucky Covington, Josh Gracin, Danny Gokey, Lauren Alaina and Scotty McCreery, as well as the country-influenced Kelly Clarkson. Meanwhile, *Nashville Star* shone a light on Kacey Musgraves, Buddy Jewell, Miranda Lambert, Chris Young, Sean Patrick McGraw and George Canyon. The teen sitcom *iCarly* launched Jennette McCurdy into the limelight, and Miley Cyrus – from country stock thanks to her dad Billy Ray Cyrus, rather than singing the stuff herself – was, of course, made famous by the Disney Channel's *Hannah Montana* (pictured).

1983–PRESENT

CARRIE UNDERWOOD

THE 'BEFORE HE CHEATS' STAR IS COUNTRY-POP ROYALTY, WITH OVER 180 INDUSTRY AWARDS AND 85 MILLION RECORDS SOLD

From Muskogee, Oklahoma, Carrie Underwood came to fame after winning *American Idol*'s fourth season in 2005. Her first single 'Inside Your Heaven' made Underwood the first solo country artist to debut at number one on the *Billboard* Hot 100, and the only one to do so in the 2000s. The same year, she released *Some Hearts* in 2005, featuring the two major singles; 'Jesus Take the Wheel' and 'Before He Cheats'. This hugely successful debut album won three Grammy Awards.

Her second album, *Carnival Ride* (2007), was also a winner, seeing Underwood take home two Grammy Awards. *Play On* followed two years later, and in 2012 she won a sixth Grammy Award for her fourth album *Blown Away*. In 2015, *Storyteller* was released to more commercial acclaim, and she did it again with 2018's *Cry Pretty*. Underwood became the first country artist to have her first five albums reach one or two on the *Billboard* 200. *Cry Pretty* also made her the only woman to top that chart with four country albums. In short, Carrie Underwood's career has been a masterclass in success.

Each album is permeated with Underwood's signature Oklahoma accent on top of country pop melodies. Not only does she have eight Grammy Awards under her belt, Underwood has also won 16 Academy of Country Music Awards and 25 Country Music Television Awards as of May 2024, making her one of the most awarded women in the country music scene, and the

> **UNDERWOOD'S CAREER HAS BEEN A MASTERCLASS IN SUCCESS**

LEFT
UNDERWOOD SHOT TO FAME AS A CONTESTANT ON THE FOURTH SEASON OF *AMERICAN IDOL*.

CARRIE UNDERWOOD

ABOVE UNDERWOOD WON BEST FEMALE COUNTRY VOCAL PERFORMANCE AND BEST NEW ARTIST GRAMMYS IN 2007.

most awarded artist overall on the CMT Awards.

In 2020, Underwood released a seventh studio album about Christmas called *My Gift*. In 2021, Underwood explored gospel music with the collection *My Savior*, where she covered popular gospel tracks. Underwood has most recently returned to her country-pop roots with the 2022 album *Denim & Rhinestones*.

UNDERWOOD EARNED COLLEGE CREDIT FOR HER MASS COMMUNICATIONS DEGREE BY APPEARING ON *AMERICAN IDOL*.

Essential Tracks

» BEFORE HE CHEATS
» JESUS TAKE THE WHEEL
» COWBOY CASANOVA

COUNTRY MUSIC ICONS

LAINEY WILSON

1992–PRESENT

Lainey Wilson

A STEADILY RISING STAR WHO HAS BEEN PIONEERING HER OWN BRAND OF "BELL-BOTTOM COUNTRY"

Lainey Wilson was born and raised in the small farming town of Baskin, Louisiana, and found herself drawn to country music from a young age. She moved to Nashville in 2011, but – as is the case for most aspiring artists – success didn't come overnight.

After years of playing small gigs and working on her songwriting, Wilson's first few records started getting her noticed, but it wasn't until 2019's *Redneck Hollywood* EP that things really started to take off. Her breakthrough single, 'Things a Man Oughta Know', topped the *Billboard* Country Airplay chart and became a popular hit on streaming services.

Things have only gone from strength to strength since then, with her 2022 album *Bell Bottom Country* becoming a Top 10 US Country hit and winning a Grammy. With her strong Southern accent and heartfelt storytelling, Wilson has received critical acclaim for her musical style, which is firmly rooted in traditional country, but has a fresh, contemporary feel.

Essential Tracks

» THINGS A MAN OUGHTA KNOW
» HEART LIKE A TRUCK
» WATERMELON MOONSHINE

IN 2023, WILSON WAS NAMED ENTERTAINER OF THE YEAR AT THE CMAS – THE SHOW'S HIGHEST HONOUR.

104 COUNTRY MUSIC ICONS

Words by Tiffany Starlow. Image Getty

MIRANDA LAMBERT

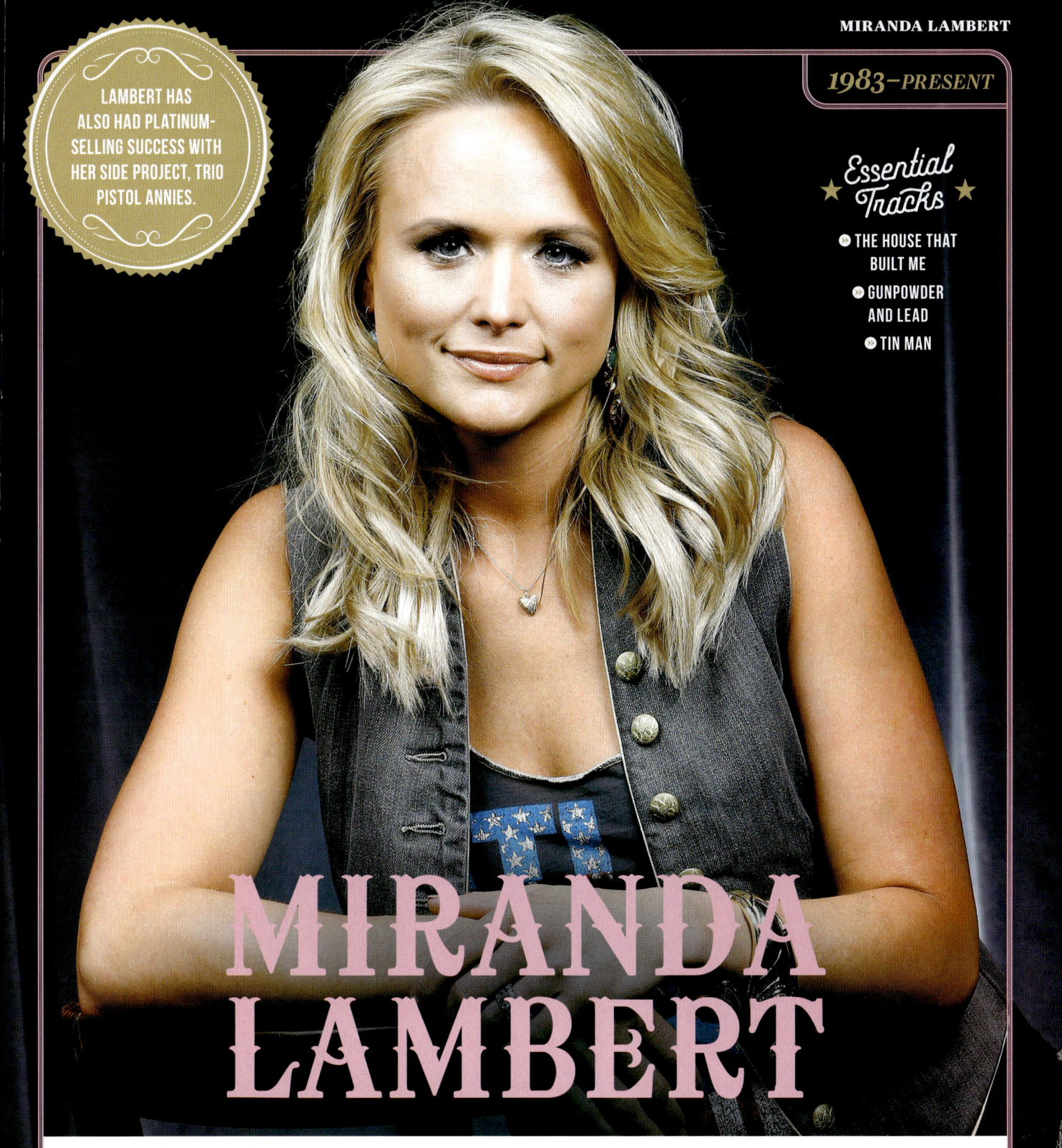

1983–PRESENT

LAMBERT HAS ALSO HAD PLATINUM-SELLING SUCCESS WITH HER SIDE PROJECT, TRIO PISTOL ANNIES.

Essential Tracks
- THE HOUSE THAT BUILT ME
- GUNPOWDER AND LEAD
- TIN MAN

ONE OF THE MOST SIGNIFICANT COUNTRY ARTISTS OF THE 21ST CENTURY AND ONE WHO HAS CHALLENGED THE STATUS QUO

Texas singer-songwriter Lambert has been a torchbearer for an exhilarating wave of strong female country voices this millennium. Lyrically, she hones in on the fine detail of working-class female lives, with wry and acute observations.

Sonically, Lambert has propelled the country sound forward with thumping digital EDM beats and big, strident, spacious mixes. But it's not at the expense of groove and feel, as is evident on 2019 No.1 hit 'Bluebird'. Her first four albums *Kerosene* (2005), *Crazy Ex-Girlfriend* (2007), *Revolution* (2009) and *Four the Record* (2011) debuted at No.1 on the US Top Country Albums chart.

It was a pattern repeated with the next four, all but *Palomino* (2022) reaching No.1 in the US Top Country charts and crossing over to reach top three spots in the US *Billboard* 200 chart. Lambert has blazed a trail for country music and invigorated the genre. In the process, she has challenged and defied country music's conventions.

1989–PRESENT

Essential Tracks
- TEARDROPS ON MY GUITAR
- TIM MCGRAW
- LOVE STORY

ONE OF SWIFT'S FIRST HITS, 'OUR SONG', WAS WRITTEN IN JUST 20 MINUTES FOR A SCHOOL TALENT SHOW.

TAYLOR SWIFT

FROM COUNTRY PRODIGY TO POP ICON: SWIFT'S FORMATIVE COUNTRY ERA DEFINED HER TRADEMARK EARNEST AND AUTOBIOGRAPHICAL SONGWRITING STYLE

A young Taylor Swift convinced her parents to move to Nashville when she was just 14 to pursue her music career. Though she has grown into one of country music's most successful crossover exports, her roots are in the vivid storytelling of the genre.

She spent the earliest days of her career touring her debut album as a support act for legends Rascal Flatts, George Strait, Brad Paisley and the joint tour of Tim McGraw and Faith Hill. After the success of her debut album, which secured Swift a series of Country Music Awards nominations, the future looked bright for the hopelessly romantic schoolgirl.

Swift began to court mainstream popularity with her second album *Fearless*, which housed mega hits 'Love Story' and 'You Belong with Me'. The album, which she began writing while on tour with Brad Paisley, secured Swift album of the year nods at the Country Music Association awards, the Academy of Country Music Awards, and the Grammys. Critics praised her trademark storytelling and catchy melodic hooks.

Her third album, *Speak Now*, continued the narrative and autobiographical songwriting that Taylor had become lauded for. Despite the ongoing discussion about the pop sensibilities of her music, *Speak Now* spawned continued success with a litany of awards and nominations in country categories.

Although her fourth album, *Red*, featured some country-tinged tracks, such as 'I Almost Do', it was clear Swift was moving firmly towards pop. She has expertly explored multiple genres over the years, including electro-pop, indie-folk and synth-pop. Despite this shift, hints of her formative musical years are present even in her more recent work, such as 'no body, no crime', and 'I Can Fix Him (No Really I Can)'.

Swift has transformed the music industry through her chart domination and her advocacy for artists' rights – notably by re-recording her first six albums over a masters ownership dispute.

LEFT AS A TEEN, SWIFT HONED HER SONGWRITING CRAFT IN NASHVILLE'S RENOWNED COUNTRY SCENE.

RIGHT SWIFT WITH HER FIRST FOUR GRAMMYS IN 2010.

1990–PRESENT

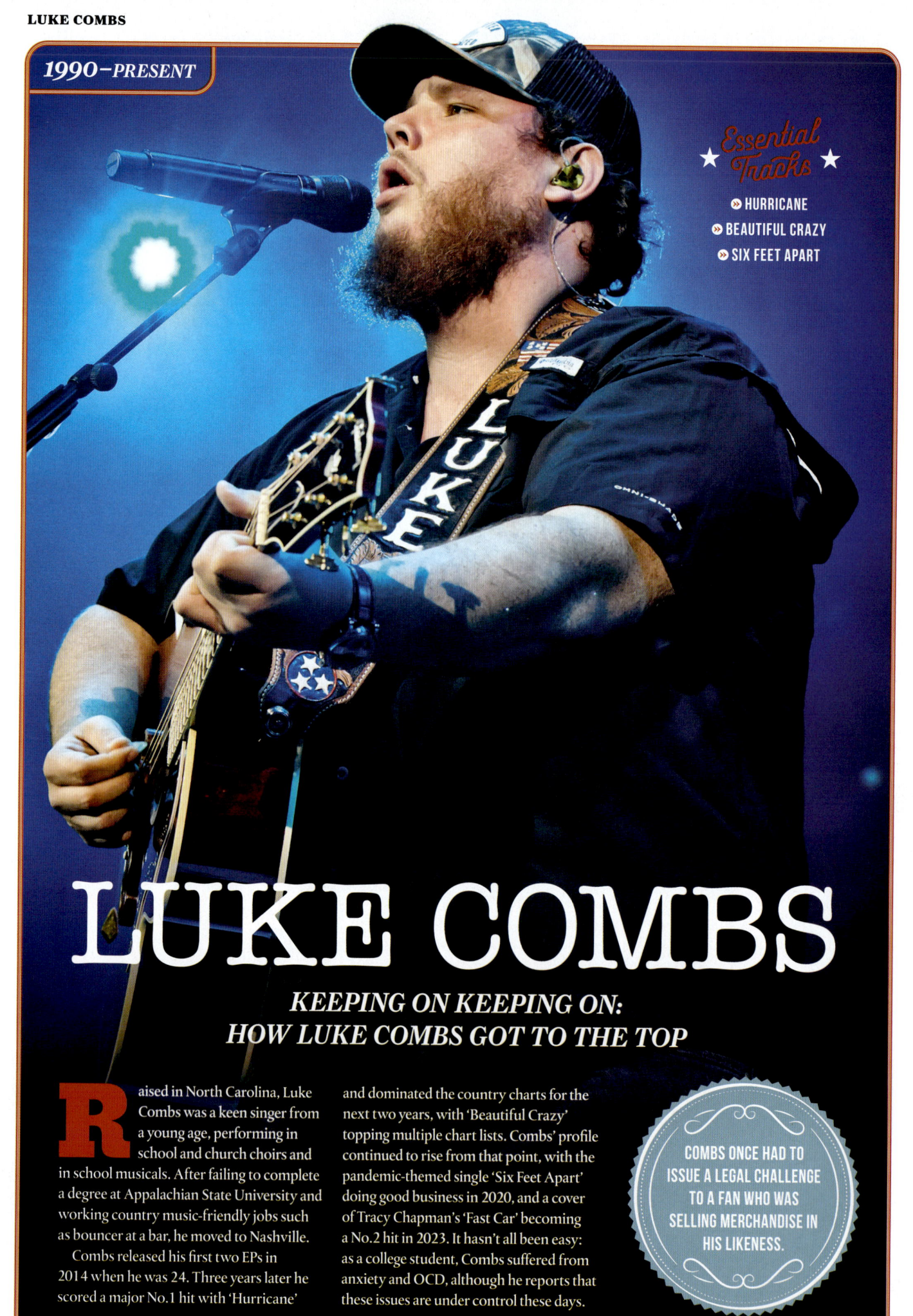

Essential Tracks
- HURRICANE
- BEAUTIFUL CRAZY
- SIX FEET APART

LUKE COMBS

KEEPING ON KEEPING ON: HOW LUKE COMBS GOT TO THE TOP

Raised in North Carolina, Luke Combs was a keen singer from a young age, performing in school and church choirs and in school musicals. After failing to complete a degree at Appalachian State University and working country music-friendly jobs such as bouncer at a bar, he moved to Nashville.

Combs released his first two EPs in 2014 when he was 24. Three years later he scored a major No.1 hit with 'Hurricane' and dominated the country charts for the next two years, with 'Beautiful Crazy' topping multiple chart lists. Combs' profile continued to rise from that point, with the pandemic-themed single 'Six Feet Apart' doing good business in 2020, and a cover of Tracy Chapman's 'Fast Car' becoming a No.2 hit in 2023. It hasn't all been easy: as a college student, Combs suffered from anxiety and OCD, although he reports that these issues are under control these days.

> COMBS ONCE HAD TO ISSUE A LEGAL CHALLENGE TO A FAN WHO WAS SELLING MERCHANDISE IN HIS LIKENESS.

ERIC CHURCH

1977–PRESENT

CHURCH WEARS SUNGLASSES ON STAGE BECAUSE HIS CONTACT LENSES TEND TO GET DRIED OUT BY BRIGHT STAGE LIGHTS.

ERIC CHURCH

TAYLOR SWIFT OWES THIS MAN A LOT. LET'S HEAR THE STORY OF THE COUNTRY CHURCH...

Born in 1977 in Granite Falls, North Carolina, the young Eric Church worked at his dad's furniture upholstery company before swapping cushions for country. At first, he played dodgy dive bars with his band the Mountain Boys, but a move to Nashville paid off and his 2006 debut album *Sinners Like Me* was well-received. Singles and tours followed, with one notable incident being the catalyst that kickstarted a certain music legend's career. Kicked off an opening slot for Rascal Flatts in '06 for playing too long despite several warnings, Church was replaced by the then newbie Taylor Swift. He joked that she should give him her first gold record as a gesture of thanks. Later, Swift actually did hand over her debut gold disc, adding the note: "Thanks for playing too long and too loud on the Flatts tour. I sincerely appreciate it. Taylor." On such small moments do entire careers depend...

★ *Essential Tracks* ★

» HOW 'BOUT YOU
» MR. MISUNDERSTOOD
» THREE YEAR OLD

COUNTRY MUSIC ICONS 109

1966–PRESENT

Essential Tracks
- THIS IS MY WORLD
- HISTORY IN THE MAKING
- ALRIGHT

RUCKER IS FRIENDS WITH GOLFER TIGER WOODS, AND SANG WITH HOOTIE & THE BLOWFISH AT HIS WEDDING.

" RUCKER'S FIRST COUNTRY ALBUM, *LEARN TO LIVE*, QUICKLY WENT GOLD AND THEN PLATINUM

DARIUS RUCKER

FROM HOOTIE & THE BLOWFISH TO COUNTRY STARDOM? YOU COULDN'T MAKE THIS STORY UP

Unlike almost anyone else, Darius Rucker built a career singing country music only after becoming a star first – in his case with the rock band Hootie & the Blowfish, with whom he is still the lead singer to this day.

Growing up in impoverished circumstances in Charleston, South Carolina, Rucker was a keen singer as a youth and formed Hootie at college in 1986. The group released their first album three years later and became stars in short order, with Rucker asked to sing the American national anthem at the World Series in 1995, performing 'The Lady Is a Tramp' with Frank Sinatra and even making a voice cameo in the TV show *Friends*.

In 2001, Rucker recorded his first solo album, an R&B effort called *The Return of Mongo Slade*. Due to contractual changes it wasn't released at the time, but was later issued by a different label under the title *Back to Then*. In 2008, he signed to Capitol Records Nashville and embarked on a parallel career as a country singer.

Rucker made his country debut with 2008's 'Don't Think I Don't Think About It', which became the first-ever No.1 single by a solo Black country artist since Charley Pride's 'Night Games' 25 years prior. His first country album, *Learn to Live*, quickly went gold and then platinum. He was also the first Black artist to win the Country Music Association's New Artist of the Year award, and indeed Rucker's career has barely slowed down since then, with six further studio albums keeping his profile high.

Like many other country artists, Rucker has successfully transitioned to TV, appearing as a mentor on *The Voice* with Blake Shelton, and has spread his remit into wider musical territory, covering a Metallica song for a 2021 project. He is also a partner in MGC Sports, an agency representing famous golfers, so if you're playing a hole sometime and you hear "Fore!" shouted in a recognisable, baritone manner, you'll know which famous artist is about to hit you.

LEFT RUCKER FIRST ROSE TO FAME IN THE NINETIES WITH ROCK BAND HOOTIE & THE BLOWFISH.

ABOVE PERFORMING AT THE GRAND OLE OPRY'S HISTORIC 5,000TH SATURDAY NIGHT BROADCAST IN 2021.

KANE BROWN

1993–PRESENT

ON 1 MAY 2019, BROWN ANNOUNCED THAT HE'D BECOME A FATHER — WHILE WALKING THE RED CARPET AT THAT YEAR'S *BILLBOARD* MUSIC AWARDS.

Essential Tracks
- CHECK YES OR NO
- USED T LOVE YOU SOBER
- WHAT IFS (WITH LAUREN ALAINA)

KANE BROWN

WANT TO BE NUMBER ONE? MEET THE COUNTRY STAR WHO HAD FIVE CHART-TOPPING TRACKS AT THE SAME TIME...

Kane Brown was raised in Georgia and Tennessee, living an itinerant childhood as his family often moved around the American South. He first performed country music at a high-school talent show and auditioned for *American Idol* and *The X Factor USA*, quitting the latter when the show tried to place him in a boy band. Instead, he uploaded songs online, gaining a following that eventually led to a breakout hit in 2015 with a cover of 'Check Yes or No' by George Strait. Major success came shortly afterwards with 2016's 'Used to Love You Sober' and a sequence of singles: he really hit the big time with the song 'What Ifs', recorded with Lauren Alaina, when it topped all five main country charts: Top Country Albums, Hot Country Songs, Country Airplay, Country Digital Song Sales and Country Streaming Songs. He's continued that success to this day, vindicating his decision not to join a reality-TV boy band once and for all.

KELSEA BALLERINI

1993–PRESENT

AN AWARD-WINNING COUNTRY-POP ARTIST, HAILING FROM KNOXVILLE, TENNESSEE, BALLERINI SIGNED HER FIRST RECORD DEAL AT JUST 19 YEARS OLD

Essential Tracks

- LOVE ME LIKE YOU MEAN IT
- THIS FEELING (WITH THE CHAINSMOKERS)
- IF YOU GO DOWN (I'M GOIN' DOWN TOO)

Kelsea BALLERINI

Kelsea Ballerini's first song, 'Love Me Like You Mean It', came out in October 2014, and was an instant hit. Success came quickly to Ballerini, who was named one of CMT's Next Women in Country later that same year. Her debut album, *The First Time*, followed in 2015. 'Love Me Like You Mean It', the album's first single, achieved number one on the *Billboard* Country Airplay Chart. Ballerini was the first solo female country artist since Carrie Underwood's 'Jesus Take the Wheel' in 2006 to gain a number one hit on a debut album. Between 2015 and 2023, Ballerini has released four studio albums which have all reached Top 5 positions in the US Country chart. Her early influences included pop artists such as Britney Spears, although she credits Taylor Swift's debut album and Shania Twain as pulling her toward country music. Ballerini boasts a wide range of featured artists, including singles with The Chainsmokers and LANY.

BALLERINI IS THE FIRST FEMALE COUNTRY ARTIST SINCE 1992 TO HAVE HER FIRST THREE SINGLES REACH NO.1.

COUNTRY MUSIC ICONS

MICKEY GUYTON

1992–PRESENT

Essential Tracks
- HEAVEN DOWN HERE
- BETTER THAN YOU LEFT ME
- BLACK LIKE ME

BREAKING DOWN BARRIERS AND PUSHING FOR CHANGE IN COUNTRY MUSIC: WELCOME, MS GUYTON

Mickey Guyton

Candace Mycale "Mickey" Guyton was born in Arlington, Texas. As a child, she moved from the local public school, where she faced racial discrimination, to a private academy. She performed in church choirs and later moved to Los Angeles to attend Santa Monica College and launch a career in music.

After working as a backing vocalist and appearing briefly on *American Idol*, she moved to Nashville and signed to Capitol Records, becoming country music's only major-label Black female artist. An early career highlight came when she performed with Kris Kristofferson, Lyle Lovett, Darius Rucker and James Taylor at the White House.

Stardom finally came her way in 2015, and the next year she was nominated for New Female Vocalist of the Year at the Academy of Country Music Awards. Her 2020 song 'Black Like Me' was well received, with CNN commenting that it "forced listeners to consider a different perspective" and her 2021 debut album, *Remember Her Name*, reached No.7 on the US Heatseekers chart.

> GUYTON'S EARLY ANXIETY OVER PRESSURES TO FIT INTO COUNTRY'S PARAMETERS LED TO A DRINKING PROBLEM, WHICH SHE SUBSEQUENTLY OVERCAME.

LADY A

FORMED 2006

UNTIL 2020, THE GROUP WERE KNOWN AS LADY ANTEBELLUM, BUT ABBREVIATED THEIR NAME TO AVOID ASSOCIATIONS WITH AMERICA'S SLAVERY ERA.

Essential Tracks

» NEVER ALONE
» NEED YOU NOW
» I RUN TO YOU

LADY A

MEET THE AWARD-WINNING TRIO THAT HELPED TO DEFINE THE POST-MILLENNIAL COUNTRY SOUND

Formed in Nashville – where else? – in 2006, Lady A is composed of singer Hillary Scott, guitarist Charles Kelley and multi-instrumentalist Dave Haywood. There are links to music heritage in the band – Scott is the daughter of the singer Linda Davis, and Kelley's brother is pop singer Josh Kelley – but when the trio debuted in 2007 as guests on a Jim Brickman song, 'Never Alone', they had a sound of their own.

They then received great acclaim as a solo entity, releasing three platinum-selling albums in a row and scoring nine No.1 singles as of May 2024, the biggest of which has been 'Need You Now', released in 2009. Awards have come thick and fast, too, starting with the trophy for Top New Duo or Group by the Academy of Country Music and New Artist of the Year by the Country Music Association in 2008. They've gone on to sell over 10 million albums in the US alone.

1988–PRESENT

KACEY MUSGRAVES

THE SEVEN-TIME GRAMMY AWARD WINNER FROM GOLDEN IS TEXAN COUNTRY WITH A MODERN POP TWIST

Kacey Musgraves started writing music in the mid-1990s when she was just eight years old. By the time she was 20, she'd self-released three solo albums and one as part of a duo called Texas Two Bits. In 2007, she placed seventh on season five of *Nashville Star*, a country singing competition. In 2012, she signed with Mercury Nashville and released the single 'Merry Go 'Round'.

What makes Musgraves stand out from traditional country artists is her progressive attitude that departs from the expected conservative traditions of previous generations. Her immaculately Texan debut album, *Same Trailer Different Park*, features the bright 'Follow Your Arrow', a song determined to show country listeners how to be themselves, acclaimed for its pro-LGBTQ+ stance. Musgraves' first album is an essential listen for any burgeoning modern country fan. It's an audio feast: close your eyes and you could be there in Texas with her. The album won a Grammy Award for the best country album in 2013.

Her second album, *Pageant Material* (2015), proved that Musgraves was here to stay as it debuted at number three on the *Billboard* 200 chart with hits such as 'Biscuits'. Third to come in 2016 was *A Very Kacey Christmas*, which eventually led to the Prime series *The Kacey Musgraves Christmas Show*. Her fourth album, 2018's *Golden Hour*, was monumental, earning Musgraves four Grammy Awards and a place in country music history.

Musgraves has never been one to shy away from the melancholic – as 2021's divorce album *Star-Crossed* proved. This was followed in 2024 by *Deeper Well*, an album full of self-awareness and growth. She has also collaborated with other artists on their songs, such as folk sensation Noah Kahan's 'She Calls Me Back'. Musgraves is keeping country alive and relevant for younger generations, and will surely continue to do so for some time to come.

LEFT IN THE TRADITIONALLY CONSERVATIVE COUNTRY GENRE, MUSGRAVES HAS BEEN AN OPENLY LIBERAL VOICE.

RIGHT MUSGRAVES WITH HER HAUL OF FOUR GRAMMYS AT THE 2019 AWARDS CEREMONY.

KACEY MUSGRAVES

Essential Tracks

» SLOW BURN
» BLOWIN' SMOKE
» DEEPER WELL

MUSGRAVES HAS WON OVER 20 INDUSTRY AWARDS SO FAR, INCLUDING THE PRESTIGIOUS ALBUM OF THE YEAR GRAMMY FOR *GOLDEN HOUR*.

" MUSGRAVES' PROGRESSIVE ATTITUDE DEPARTS FROM THE EXPECTED CONSERVATIVE TRADITIONS OF PREVIOUS GENERATIONS

Morgan Wallen

1993–PRESENT

Essential Tracks
- WHISKEY GLASSES
- CHASIN' YOU
- I HAD SOME HELP

NO STRANGER TO CONTROVERSY, WALLEN HAS PREVIOUSLY BEEN CRITICISED FOR USE OF A RACIAL SLUR AND IGNORING COVID GUIDELINES.

THE BAD BOY OF COUNTRY, MORGAN WALLEN HAS THE TUNES – AND THE HAIRCUT – TO PAY THE BILLS

Morgan Wallen was born and raised in Tennessee and switched to music after an injury cut short his high school baseball career. He first emerged into the public eye in 2014 after competing on *The Voice*, after which industry connections were forged and he launched a solo career. A debut EP in 2015 went gold and he signed to Big Loud Records, who began releasing his material two years later. In 2018 he made the courageous decision to grow a mullet and immediately gained an appreciative following among country fans nostalgic for 80s chic, helped along by partying-themed singles such as 'Whiskey Glasses' and 'Chasin' You'. *Billboard* magazine ran the cover headline 'Is Morgan Wallen Country's Next Global Star?' in 2020 and was soon proven correct, as his three albums to date have all been huge hits. His latest single, 'I Had Some Help', featured the rapper Post Malone and came out as we went to press.

CHRIS STAPLETON

1978–PRESENT

Essential Tracks
- TRAVELLER
- IF HE AIN'T GONNA LOVE YOU (WITH JAKE OWEN)
- TENNESSEE WHISKEY

CHRIS STAPLETON

AWARDS MIGHT AS WELL BE CHRIS STAPLETON'S MIDDLE NAME, AS HE HAS FOUND SUCCESS BOTH SOLO AND AS A PROLIFIC COLLABORATOR

Chris Stapleton was born in Lexington, Kentucky and moved to Nashville to study engineering, which is a bit like moving to Las Vegas to study biology. Still, he soon dropped out of college to make music – a wise move as he's now released several No.1 songs and has over 170 solo and collaborative compositions under his belt. He's a prolific writer for other artists, including Kenny Chesney, Luke Bryan, George Strait and Tim McGraw to name a few, and has ventured outside the country realm writing for Adele, P!nk, Sheryl Crow and Justin Timberlake. His solo work has also been successful, with 2015's *Traveller* going quadruple platinum and scoring a rare diamond certification for a version of the often-covered 'Tennessee Whiskey'. Stapleton's trophy room must be a large one: it contains over 70 awards, including many from the Grammys, the Academy of Country Music, and the Country Music Association.

IN 2023, ROLLING STONE INCLUDED STAPLETON AT NO.170 ON ITS LIST OF THE 200 GREATEST SINGERS OF ALL TIME.

ACTIVE *1999–2021*

★ Essential Tracks ★

- BLESS THE BROKEN ROAD
- WHAT HURTS THE MOST
- LIFE IS A HIGHWAY

RASCAL FLATTS

A LONG-LASTING, HIGHLY ACCLAIMED TRIO THAT PUSHED COUNTRY-ROCK INTO THE NOUGHTIES MAINSTREAM

Founded in 1999 in Nashville, Rascal Flatts were a country band comprising Gary LeVox on lead vocals, his second cousin Jay DeMarcus on bass and Joe Don Rooney on guitar. Since their debut single, 'Prayin' for Daylight' in 2000, the trio became highly popular among fans of smoothly produced country-rock.

Their six-album run for the Disney-owned Lyric Street Records label ran from 2000 to 2010, after which point the group switched to Big Machine Records (the erstwhile home of Taylor Swift and other artists) for five more albums, calling time in 2017 with *Back to Us* and officially disbanding in 2021.

The trio had a great run by any standards. Over the decades they released more than 40 singles, a startling 16 of which hit No.1 on various US and/or Canadian charts: you'll almost certainly know one or more of their three biggest hits, a cover of Marcus Hummon's 'Bless the Broken Road', 'What Hurts the Most' and a version of Tom Cochrane's 'Life Is a Highway' that appeared on the soundtrack of *Cars* in 2006.

Rascal Flatts also secured a huge amount of awards for the band's mantelpiece, including Top Vocal Group by the Academy of Country Music from 2003 to 2009, and the Vocal Group of the Year award by the Country Music Association in every year from 2003 to 2008. The group received a star on the Hollywood Walk of Fame in 2012, scored a Grammy for 'Bless the Broken Road' and became sought-after producers: DeMarcus has gone on to work on albums by Chicago and more.

Given all that, why did the trio decide to go their separate ways? Well, all three men were in their late forties or early fifties when the split came, and perhaps there's only so much country-rockin' the average singer can comfortably handle in one lifetime. Add a few personal problems here and there, plus the small matter of the pandemic, and perhaps a split was inevitable. Still, their recorded catalogue isn't going anywhere, so hit play and enjoy.

> **THE TRIO BECAME HIGHLY POPULAR AMONG FANS OF SMOOTHLY PRODUCED COUNTRY-ROCK**

THE GROUP MADE MANY VISITS AND DONATED MILLIONS TO THE MONROE CARELL JR CHILDREN'S HOSPITAL IN NASHVILLE, WHERE A SURGERY CENTRE WAS NAMED IN THEIR HONOUR IN 2010.

ALLISON RUSSELL

1982–PRESENT

Essential Tracks
- NIGHTFLYER
- THE RETURNER
- EVE WAS BLACK

INFUSING COUNTRY WITH BLUES, STRINGS, AND GOSPEL, ALLISON RUSSELL CREATES POWERFUL AND ETHEREAL MUSIC

Canadian-born multi-instrumentalist and singer-songwriter Allison Russell blends together her activism and artistry to create compelling and soulful music.

Her earliest releases were as a part of groups – Po' Girls, and later Our Native Daughters. Her debut solo album *Outside Child* drew on her experiences overcoming a childhood with an abusive and white supremacist stepfather. The follow-up album, *The Returner*, has a celebratory feel: something Russell describes as the undervalued "survivor's joy". Both albums earned a string of awards nominations.

Her music is heavily influenced by her activism: notably a powerful and Grammy-winning performance of 'Eve Was Black'. She is backed by the Rainbow Coalition (an all-femme musician collective), has been a vocal supporter of minority groups, and organised benefits in response to anti-LGBTQ+ legislation. Russell is a part of country music's new frontier: a modernisation of who represents the genre, unconfined by gender, sexuality or race.

OUTSIDE CHILD TOOK JUST FOUR DAYS TO RECORD, WITH ALL TRACKS PERFORMED LIVE BY THE FULL BAND.

MAREN MORRIS

1990–PRESENT

MORRIS IN SUPERGROUP THE HIGHWOMEN, NAMED IN HONOUR OF JOHNNY CASH AND WILLIE NELSON'S SUPERGROUP, THE HIGHWAYMEN.

MAREN MORRIS

WITH HER AWARD-WINNING MUSICAL STYLINGS, MORRIS IS BRINGING COUNTRY MUSIC TO NEW AUDIENCES

Morris began her career at age 15. After initially struggling to find success – including being rejected from TV talent shows like *American Idol* – she moved to Nashville on the advice of Kacey Musgraves.

Once in Nashville, her career picked up pace and she began a promising career in songwriting – including songs for country icons such as Tim McGraw and pop legend Kelly Clarkson. Morris' debut album, *Hero*, launched her singing career, winning her the CMA Awards' New Artist of the Year honour, alongside a string of other industry nominations.

Morris has been credited with helping modernise country music. Personally, she has been outspoken against racism, misogyny and homophobia. Influenced by the early 2000s pop and hip-hop, her sound is a contemporary country that is incisive and witty. Morris has lent her country-tinged writing and vocals to a wide range of artists in collaborations – from folk's Hozier and pop's Taylor Swift, to dance's Zedd and Grey.

Essential Tracks

- MY CHURCH
- THE BONES
- I COULD USE A LOVE SONG

COUNTRY MUSIC ICONS 123

ZAC BROWN BAND

ZAC BROWN BAND

FORMED 2002

AS OF MAY 2024, THE ZAC BROWN BAND HAS RECEIVED NO FEWER THAN 55 AWARD NOMINATIONS.

Essential Tracks
- GOODBYE IN HER EYES
- HOMEGROWN
- MY OLD MAN

DAVE GROHL AND JOHN VARVATOS LIKE THE ZAC BROWN BAND – WHAT MORE OF A RECOMMENDATION DO YOU NEED?

Zac Brown grew up in Georgia and became interested in bluegrass music as a kid while jamming with his father and brother. In high school, he played solo gigs and by his twenties, he was touring the American South.

In 2002 he put together the Zac Brown Band and founded a label called Southern Ground. The first ZBB album, *Home Grown*, was released in 2004, and four years later success came their way with a deal with Sony Nashville and a hit single called 'Chicken Fried'. *Billboard* voted the band's 2012 record *Uncaged* as the best country release of the year, and the group really broke into the mainstream when Foo Fighter Dave Grohl recorded them for one of his eponymous sessions in 2013. Shortly afterwards, Brown announced a partnership with the rock'n'roll stylist John Varvatos, perhaps the truest indication to date that the future is bright for Brown and his fellow musicians.

COUNTRY MUSIC ICONS

1976–PRESENT

LUKE BRYAN

Essential Tracks
- ALL MY FRIENDS SAY
- TAKE MY DRUNK ASS HOME
- RAIN IS A GOOD THING

THE STORY OF THE MULTI-MILLIONAIRE SINGER, TV PERSONALITY AND ENTHUSIASTIC BEER FAN

THE UNEXPECTED DEATHS OF BRYAN'S OLDER BROTHER AND SISTER HELPED BRYAN CONNECT WITH HIS 2013 SINGLE 'DRINK A BEER'.

Born on a peanut farm in Leesburg, Georgia, Luke Bryan made the necessary career move to Nashville in 2001, having studied business at college first. This education would have proven useful when his career as a songwriter and then a performer took off after he hit big with the 2007 single 'All My Friends Say'.

His preferred subject matter – various ways of having fun – was immediately popular among young country audiences, who snapped up songs such as 'We Rode in Trucks', 'Sorority Girls' and 'Take My Drunk Ass Home', although some critics dismissed this relatively simple stuff with the 'bro-country' tag. This didn't slow Bryan down, however, and he has gone on to release a series of high-charting, huge-selling singles, EPs and albums. He also appeared on the April 2010 episode of *Celebrity Apprentice* and became a judge on *American Idol* seven years later, thus transcending the country niche and entering mainstream culture.

1976–PRESENT

SHELTON IS A PROLIFIC CHARITY DONOR. EXAMPLES INCLUDE $20,000 TO WILDLIFE CAUSES AND $150,000 TO FOOD BANKS DURING COVID.

BLAKE SHELTON

ONE OF THE BIGGEST NAMES IN COUNTRY MUSIC OF ANY ERA AND STYLE: IT'S MR SHELTON

BLAKE SHELTON

RIGHT SHELTON MARRIED GWEN STEFANI IN JULY 2021 AND IS STEPFATHER TO HER THREE SONS.

SHELTON HAS SOLD OVER 10 MILLION ALBUMS AND MORE THAN 30 MILLION SINGLES

LEFT ON STAGE AT THE 2005 CMA MUSIC FESTIVAL IN NASHVILLE.

Blake Shelton was born in Ada, Oklahoma and – like so many other future stars – he was singing and playing the guitar by his teens. At the age of 16, he received Oklahoma's Denbo Diamond Award, a trophy given by the state to promising new entertainers, and he swiftly relocated to Nashville to forge a career as a musician. A deal with Sony followed and his 2001 debut album, a self-titled affair, eventually went platinum.

Since then Shelton's career has remained at the very top end of the commercial music industry, with a long sequence of successful albums keeping his profile high: he has accrued an astounding list of over 100 industry awards, including gongs from the Country Music Association, Country Music Television, the Academy of Country Music, Broadcast Music Inc, and the American Society of Composers, Authors, and Publishers. Later, when he joined the panel on *The Voice*, he was given the NATPE Reality Breakthrough Award for Best Reality Personality. On top of these honours, he has sold over 10 million albums and more than 30 million singles – numbers that only the biggest country stars can match.

Proof that country musicians can dominate mainstream headlines even if their surname is not Swift came in 2015, when Shelton announced that he was dating his fellow judge from *The Voice*, singer Gwen Stefani of No Doubt fame. Both partners were enduring high-profile divorces at the time, a fact which Shelton noted: "Gwen saved my life. Who else on Earth could understand going through a high-profile divorce from another musician? You can't even imagine the similarities in our divorces."

Despite retiring from *The Voice* in 2022, Shelton continues to release new music and perform on tours. He also runs a chain of restaurants called Ole Red, making him the perfect example of the modern country-music businessperson.

Essential Tracks

- AUSTIN
- THE BABY
- PLAYBOYS OF THE SOUTHWESTERN WORLD

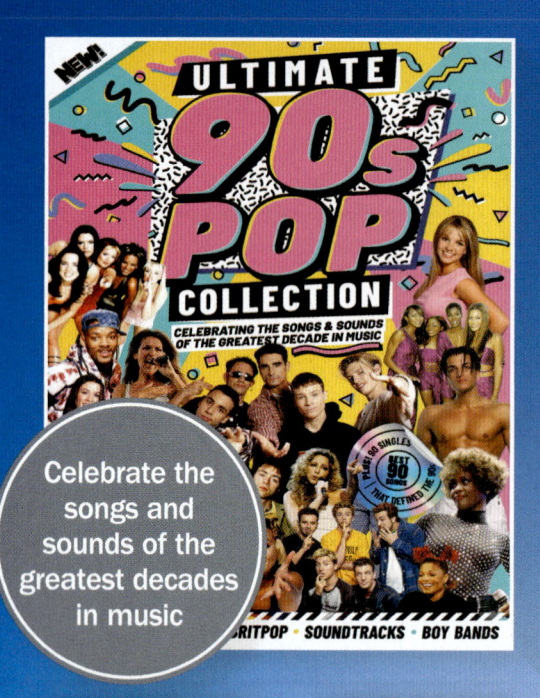

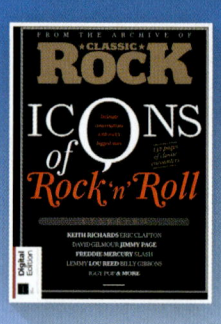

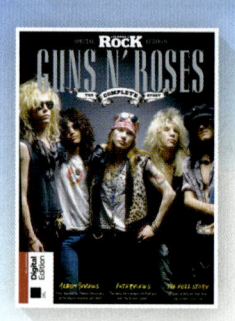

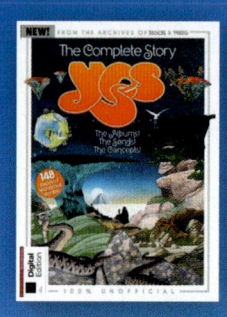

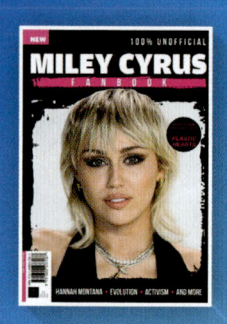

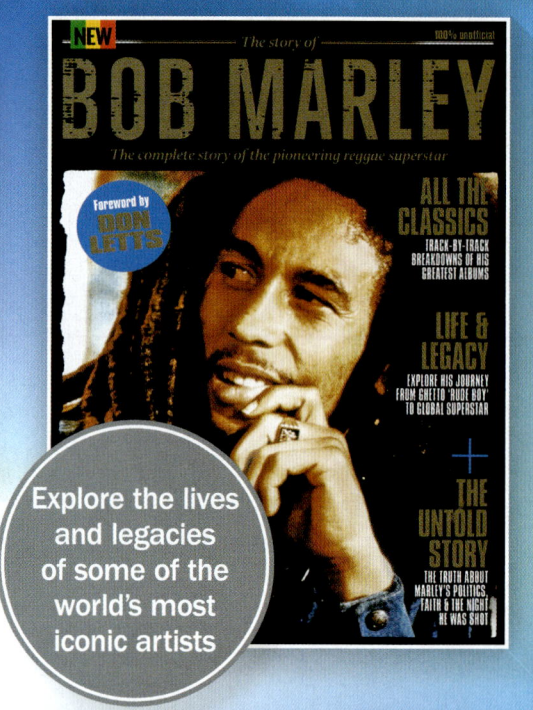

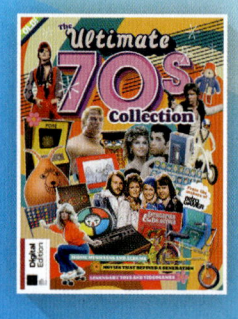

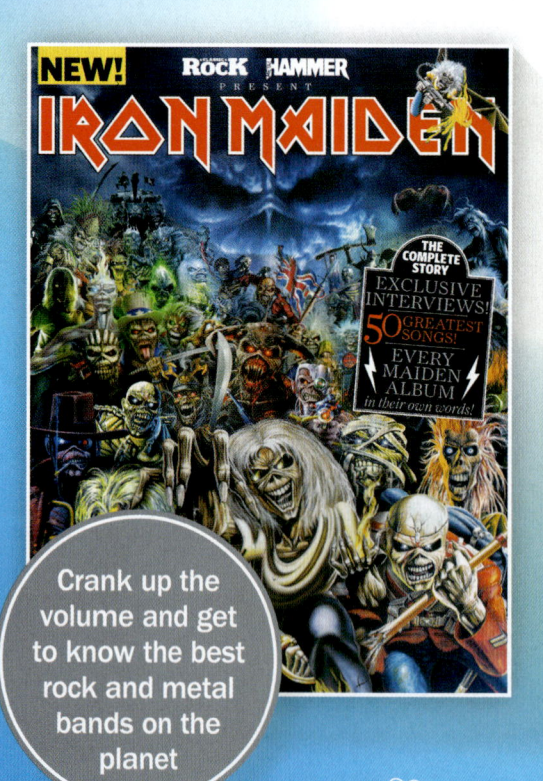

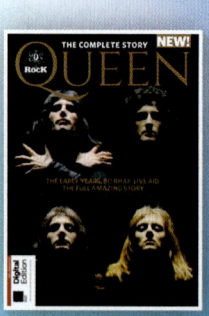

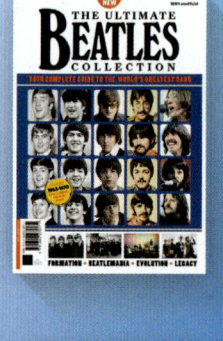

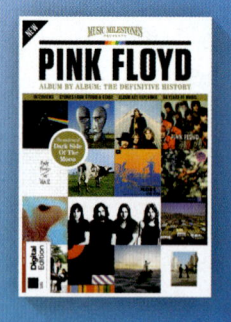

Celebrate the songs and sounds of the greatest decades in music

Explore the lives and legacies of some of the world's most iconic artists

Crank up the volume and get to know the best rock and metal bands on the planet

✓ Get great savings when you buy direct from us

✓ 1000s of great titles, many not available anywhere else

✓ World-wide delivery and super-safe ordering

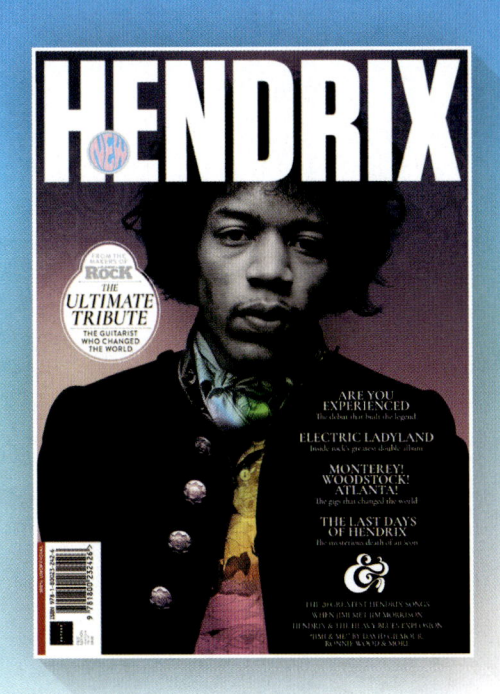

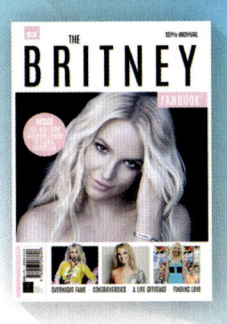

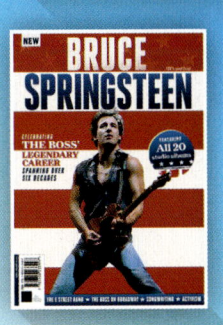

ROCK ON WITH OUR MUSIC BOOKAZINES

Discover the origins of legendary songs, relive iconic performances and meet the pioneers behind some of music's greatest names

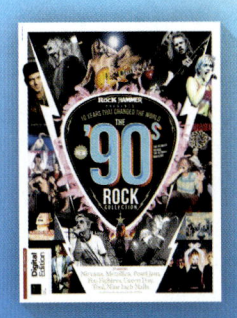

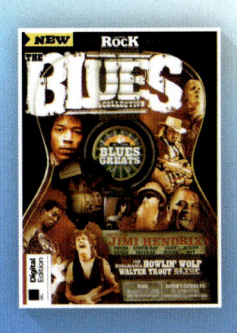

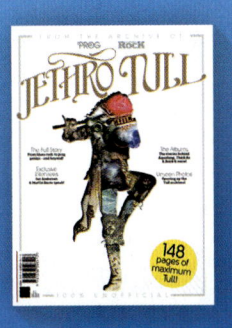

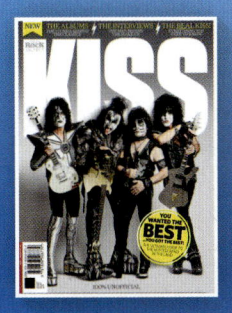

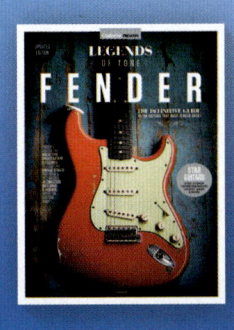

Discover everything there is to know about your favourite pop stars

Follow us on Instagram @futurebookazines

www.magazinesdirect.com
Magazines, back issues & bookazines.

FUTURE

COUNTRY MUSIC ICONS

Future PLC Quay House, The Ambury, Bath, BA1 1UA

Editorial
Editor **Jacqueline Snowden**
Art Editor **Lora Barnes**
Head of Art & Design **Greg Whitaker**
Editorial Director **Jon White**
Managing Director **Grainne McKenna**

Contributors
Grace Almond, Neil Crossley, Andy Downes, Farrah Frost,
April Madden, Dan Peel, Dave Smith, Kate Waldock

Cover images
Alamy, Getty Images

Photography
Alamy, Getty Images
All copyrights and trademarks are recognised and respected

Advertising
Media packs are available on request
Commercial Director **Clare Dove**

International
Head of Print Licensing **Rachel Shaw**
licensing@futurenet.com
www.futurecontenthub.com

Circulation
Head of Newstrade **Tim Mathers**

Production
Head of Production **Mark Constance**
Production Project Manager **Matthew Eglinton**
Advertising Production Manager **Joanne Crosby**
Digital Editions Controller **Jason Hudson**
Production Managers **Keely Miller, Nola Cokely,
Vivienne Calvert, Fran Twentyman**

Printed in the UK

Distributed by Marketforce – www.marketforce.co.uk
For enquiries, please email: mfcommunications@futurenet.com

Country Music Icons First Edition (MUB6127)
© 2024 Future Publishing Limited

We are committed to only using magazine paper which is derived from responsibly managed, certified forestry and chlorine-free manufacture. The paper in this bookazine was sourced and produced from sustainable managed forests, conforming to strict environmental and socioeconomic standards.

All contents © 2024 Future Publishing Limited or published under licence. All rights reserved. No part of this magazine may be used, stored, transmitted or reproduced in any way without the prior written permission of the publisher. Future Publishing Limited (company number 2008885) is registered in England and Wales. Registered office: Quay House, The Ambury, Bath BA1 1UA. All information contained in this publication is for information only and is, as far as we are aware, correct at the time of going to press. Future cannot accept any responsibility for errors or inaccuracies in such information. You are advised to contact manufacturers and retailers directly with regard to the price of products/services referred to in this publication. Apps and websites mentioned in this publication are not under our control. We are not responsible for their contents or any other changes or updates to them. This magazine is fully independent and not affiliated in any way with the companies mentioned herein.

Future Connectors. Creators. Experience Makers.

Future plc is a public company quoted on the London Stock Exchange (symbol: FUTR)
www.futureplc.com

Chief Executive Officer **Jon Steinberg**
Non-Executive Chairman **Richard Huntingford**
Chief Financial and Strategy Officer **Penny Ladkin-Brand**

Tel +44 (0)1225 442 244